Flat-Footed Truths

Flat-Footed Truths

TELLING BLACK WOMEN'S LIVES

Edited and with an Introduction by

Patricia Bell-Scott

with Juanita Johnson-Bailey

An Owl Book

Henry Holt and Company ı New York

Henry Holt and Company, Inc.
Publishers since 1866
115 West 18th Street
New York, New York 10011

Henry Holt® is a registered trademark
of Henry Holt and Company, Inc.

Library of Congress Cataloging-in-Publication Data
Flat-footed truths: telling Black women's lives / edited and with an
introduction by Patricia Bell-Scott, with Juanita Johnson-Bailey.
p.   cm.
ISBN 0-8050-4629-1
1. Minority women—United States—Social conditions.   2. Afro-
American women—Social conditions.   3. Afro-American women—
Biography.   4. Women, Black—United States—Social conditions.
I. Bell-Scott, Patricia.   II. Johnson-Bailey, Juanita.
HQ1154.F55   1998   97-35108
305.48'896073—dc21   CIP

Henry Holt books are available for special promotions and
premiums. For details contact: Director, Special Markets.

First published in hardcover in 1998 by
Henry Holt and Company, Inc.

First Owl Books Edition 1999

Designed by Michelle McMillian

Printed in the United States of America

1o

·eviously

We can simply refuse to leave our children unarmed with the truth as we have experienced it. . . . Love is best expressed through truth.

—Alice Walker

CONTENTS

PART II: CLAIMING LIVES LOST

PART III: TELLING LIVES AS RESISTANCE

PART IV: TELLING LIVES AS TRANSFORMATION

ACKNOWLEDGMENTS

This book exists in large part because of the unwavering commitment of Charlotte Sheedy; the patience and encouragement of Tracy A. Sherrod; the mother/sister love of Dorothy Wilbanks, Brenda F. Bell, and Georgia M. Johnson; the wisdom and inspiration of Sapphire; the spiritual writings of Alice Walker and Ana Castillo; the research and clerical assistance of Angela Humphrey Brown, April Few, and Chelita Edwards; and the support of Arvin Scott, Marvin Bailey, and Brandice E. A. Bailey. We also thank Maya Angelou, whose *I Know Why the Caged Bird Sings* gives so many the courage to speak.

FOREWORD

marcia ann gillespie

How do we tell our life stories? Do we begin in the here and now? Where do our stories begin and those of our foremothers end? A church song I've always loved proclaims, "My soul looks back in wonder, how I got over." When I try to make sense of this life of mine and my times, I remember the stories told to me of Lavinia Risen, my maternal great-grandmother. As a child I fell in love with her, partly because I knew that I looked like her.

From early childhood I peppered my grandmother with questions about her mother, a woman born in slavery, who came into womanhood as someone's chattel. So many of my questions remained unanswered or only partly answered, and the answers never satisfied me even when I was a child. Then as now I wanted to—no, hungered to know Lavinia Risen's life story. I wanted to know her, what she'd experienced and endured, her pleasures and pains in slavery and in freedom. I savored the few details that my grandmother shared—more as

I grew older, but never enough. I know that she was a slave on a plantation in Ashland, Virginia, that she bore several children while still held in bondage, that they were the children of the overseer or maybe the plantation owner. That when slavery ended she left that place with her babies and made her way to Richmond, Virginia. That Lavinia Risen became Lavinia Temple when she married my great-grandfather. That together they had many more children. That he was a butcher and they were relatively prosperous, but the marriage soured and she gathered her children—all of the younger ones and all of the older ones who chose to go with her—and moved north to Long Branch, New Jersey, where she leased a farm. That while in Long Branch she beat a White man into the ground after he had assaulted one of her children and that she taught my great-uncle Larry Young, who would become a somewhat successful prizefighter at the turn of the century, how to box. But even as a three-braided little colored girl, I knew when I first heard of her that I had no more than a sketchy outline of her life—that there was so much more.

I try to imagine what she must have been like. I long to know her thoughts and hopes and dreams. How she got over. But there are no journals, no diaries, no letters. She never learned to read or write more than her name. I have only the fragmented memories that my now long-dead grandmother shared with me and with my mother and aunt.

Her life remains shrouded in silence, as do the lives of the overwhelming majority of the women who have come before us, women whose sentinel spirits stride alongside us as we journey forth. But the silence of women, the silencing of so many women, of far too many of our foremothers, leaves us wondering, always wondering, what secrets, what practical advice and hard-earned wisdom, they might have shared with us. Wondering how like or unlike them we are, how much our lives differ. Women sharing their life stories enrich us all, and we hunger for the connection, often unknowingly. These "home truths" resounded in my soul as I read this collection. Reading Alice Walker, I was transported back to the early 1970s to a Black women's conference in Boston. There I sat along with a roomful of sister congregants, all of us listening, raptly, intensely, most of us with tears streaming down our cheeks, as Alice softly read "In Search of Our Mother's Gardens" to our group. There was so much longing and relief, grief and joy, in our silent tears: relief that the silence was being breached, longing for all the life stories forever silenced. We were grieving with and for our foremothers for the creativity so many were unable to express and jubilating in our sister Alice's affirmation of the triumph of the spirit. I don't know whether Patricia Bell-Scott was in that room on that special day, but in assembling this powerful collection with Juanita Johnson-Bailey, she addresses the feelings we shared in that room that long-ago day.

She knows, as do all the women who contributed to this book, that acknowledging our longing to know and share women's life stories and to tell our own pushes us to break the silence. Sometimes we do it as bell hooks describes in "Writing Autobiography," as an act of personal therapy—to affirm our existence, to save our sanity or our very lives. Or to bear witness. Or to help clear the road, as Audre Lorde did for those who have been made to feel that their very being is unacceptable, dangerous, or under siege. Often it's like being adrift in the middle of the sea and shooting a flare out in the deep dark—a prayer that we are not alone.

When we share our stories and seek to unshroud the lives of women who have come before us, the telling empowers us all.

We connect the dots between the personal and the political; the individual's truths and the larger realities; women's existence, our people's journey, and the human experience. It can be a painful process, challenging our integrity at every turn as we confront painful truths, less than flattering aspects of our lives and/or the lives of others, and push the bounds of privacy. Are we censoring ourselves in order to maintain the illusion that all of us are brave, that all Black women are strong? How much do we want to know or tell? What to keep? What to share?

The sister writers in this wonderful collection have struggled with all of these questions and more as they set about writing their stories or exploring the lives of others. Having chosen to break the silence, each of them has also chosen to be brave rather than popular, honest rather than facile. And each of them has endured the wrath of those who choose to cling to stereotypes or fairy tales about women's lives or celebrate only those stories that affirm their scripted notions of what our lives should mean and reflect. Perhaps, like me, they carry a face or a name buried deep in their hearts that speaks to their spirits, exhorting them to pull the gags out of their mouths, tell their stories, and help give voice to ours.

As the editor of a feminist magazine and the former editor of a Black women's magazine, I know why I do what I do. Lavinia Risen's silence speaks to me, has spoken to me all my life. I seek to share women's life stories, women's words, because I want to know "how we got over." *Flat-Footed Truths: Telling Black Women's Lives*, edited by Patricia Bell-Scott with Juanita Johnson-Bailey, reminds us all that we get there by daring to speak truth to power.

TELLING FLAT-FOOTED TRUTHS:
AN INTRODUCTION

patricia bell-scott

I am haunted by the photograph of a two-year-old girl seated in what appears to me to be a place too lonesome for a child. Although I am taken with the beauty of her round face, plump limbs, and soft, shiny hair, I am bothered by the apprehension in her eyes. At times I am so unsettled by her image that I remove the photograph from view—wanting to avoid the truths her eyes tell. These truths are of a child ever hungry for the love of a mother who never stopped grieving the untimely death of another daughter, and of an ambitious girl whose dreams are shattered in the segregated South of the 1940s. Despite my discomfort, the wish to evade this photograph is only momentary. I always retrieve it and place it in the brightest of light, where her kindness and, most important, her survival outshine the circumstances of life. I am blessed to know this child, for she is my mother. And she has taught me that truth—sometimes beautiful, sometimes ugly—is ultimately healing.

In Her Chair (circa 1930), Dorothy Graves. This photograph was taken in Chattanooga, Tennessee, when Dorothy Graves Wilbanks, mother of Patricia Bell-Scott, was approximately two years old. This chair, one of her favorite childhood objects, represents a place all her own. Photographer unidentified, personal collection of Patricia Bell-Scott.

This book is about the *process* of telling Black women's lives, with an eye toward what folks in my southern Black community call "flat-footed truths." To tell the flat-footed truth means to offer a story or statement that is straightforward, unshakable, and unembellished. This kind of truth-telling, especially by and about Black women, can be risky business because our lives are often devalued and our voices periodically silenced. But there have always been women who insist on speaking truths in the face of disbelief and public criticism (from within *and* outside of African American communities). And it is to them—women like Sojourner Truth, who, although she could neither read nor write, convinced a judge that she was the mother of a son who had been sold into slavery; Audre Lorde, who urged Black women to resist all forms of oppression and claim the whole of our lives; Anita F. Hill, who brought the ugliness of sexual harassment to a national audience before the incredulous gaze of the U.S. Senate Judiciary Committee; and the majority of ordinary sisters who struggle daily for the sweetness of personal autonomy—that this book is dedicated.

Flat-Footed Truths is a collection of essays, interviews, poetry, and photographic images in which African American women writers and artists tell lives through their chosen medium. It is designed as an extended conversation that covers four major themes. Part I discusses the challenge of telling one's own life; Part II, the adventure of claiming lives neglected or lost; Part III, the affirmation of lives of resistance; and Part IV, the optimism and healing of lives transformed. In recognition of the fact that the visual arts historically preceded formal writing as a means of recording life experience, each section is introduced by a photographic image that captures and distills some aspect or period of a woman's life.

It is our hope that this book, the first to focus explicitly on the process of telling Black women's lives, will find its way into the hands of general readers interested in Black and women's autobiography, that students and teachers in Black and women's literature and history will find it helpful, and that writers and creative artists who use (or aspire to use) the truths of our lives as fuel for their work might find it encouraging. We also hope that *Flat-Footed Truths* will nourish another generation of writers, artists, and thinkers who will uncover the layers of our experience and stand us in the light so that our beauty can be seen, our souls healed, and our lives transformed.

PART I

TELLING ONE'S OWN LIFE

I moved what waz my unconscious knowledge of being in a colored woman's body to my known everydayness.

—NTOZAKE SHANGE

Self-Portraits (1990), Gilda Snowden. *Self-Portraits* is a hypnotic pastel drawing that mirrors the form of Gilda Snowden, a Detroit native who specializes in painting and mixed-media constructions. An abstract expressionist, Snowden feels that art must tell a story and that her work presents the world idealistically, "transforming the imperfect into something perfect." She attributes the sense of movement and vibrancy in her art to the urban realities of her childhood in Detroit. Photographer, Dirk Bakker, © The Detroit Institute of Arts.

IF YOU LOSE YOUR PEN

ruth forman

and all you find is a broken pencil on the floor
and the pencil has no sharpener
and the sharpener is in the store
and your pocket has no money

and if you look again
and all you find is a black Bic
and the Bic you need is green

and if it appears beneath the mattress of your couch
but the couch is dirty and you suddenly want to clean
beneath the pillows
but you have no vacuum and the vacuum is in the store
and your pocket has no money

it is not your pen you are looking for

it is your tongue and those who speak with it
your grandmothers and doves and ebony spiders
hovering the corners of your throat

it is your tongue
and if you cannot find your tongue
do not go looking for the cat
you know you will not find her
she is in the neighbor's kitchen eating Friskies
she is in the neighbor's yard making love

if you cannot find your tongue do not look for it
for you are so busy looking it cannot find you
the doves are getting dizzy and your grandmothers annoyed
be still and let them find you
they will come when they are ready

and when they are
it will not matter if your pockets are empty
if you write with a green Bic or a black Bic
or the blood of your finger
you will write
you will write

WRITING AUTOBIOGRAPHY

bell hooks

To me, telling the story of my growing up years was intimately connected with the longing to kill the self I was without really having to die. I wanted to kill that self in writing. Once that self was gone—out of my life forever—I could more easily become the me of me. It was clearly the Gloria Jean of my tormented and anguished childhood that I wanted to be rid of, the girl who was always wrong, always punished, always subjected to some humiliation or other, always crying, the girl who was to end up in a mental institution because she could not be anything but crazy, or so they told her. She was the girl who sat a hot iron on her arm pleading with them to leave her alone, the girl who wore her scar as a brand marking her madness. Even now I can hear the voices of my sisters saying "mama make Gloria stop crying." By writing the autobiography, it was not just this Gloria I would be rid of, but the past that had a hold on me, that kept me from the present. I wanted not to forget the past but to break its hold. This death in writing was to be liberatory.

Until I began to try and write an autobiography, I thought that it would be a simple task this telling of one's story. And yet I tried year after year, never writing more than a few pages. My inability to write out the story I interpreted as an indication that I was not ready to let go of the past, that I was not ready to be fully in the present. Psychologically, I considered the possibility that I had become attached to the wounds and sorrows of my childhood, that I held to them in a manner that blocked my efforts to be self-realized, whole, to be healed. A key message in Toni Cade Bambara's novel *The Salteaters*, which tells the story of Velma's suicide attempt, her breakdown, is expressed when the healer asks her "are you sure sweetheart, that you want to be well?"

There was very clearly something blocking my ability to tell my story. Perhaps it was remembered scoldings and punishments when mama heard me saying something to a friend or stranger that she did not think should be said. Secrecy and silence— these were central issues. Secrecy about family, about what went on in the domestic household was a bond between us—was part of what made us family. There was a dread one felt about breaking that bond. And yet I could not grow inside the atmosphere of secrecy that had pervaded our lives and the lives of other families about us. Strange that I had always challenged the secrecy, always let something slip that should not be known growing up, yet as a writer staring into the solitary space of paper, I was bound, trapped in the fear that a bond is lost or broken in the telling. I did not want to be the traitor, the teller of family secrets—and yet I wanted to be a writer. Surely, I told myself, I could write a purely imaginative work—a work that would not hint at personal private realities. And so I tried. But always there were the intruding traces, those elements of real life however disguised. Claiming the freedom to grow as an imaginative writer was connected for me with having the courage to open, to be able to tell the truth of one's life as I had experienced it in writing. To talk about one's life—that I could do. To write about it, to leave a trace—that was frightening.

The longer it took me to begin the process of writing auto-biography, the further removed from those memories I was becoming. Each year, a memory seemed less and less clear. I wanted not to lose the vividness, the recall, and felt an urgent need to begin the work and complete it. Yet I could not begin even though I had begun to confront some of the reasons I was blocked, as I am blocked just now in writing this piece because I am afraid to express in writing the experience that served as a catalyst for that block to move.

I had met a young Black man. We were having an affair. It is important that he was Black. He was in some mysterious way a link to this past that I had been struggling to grapple with, to name in writing. With him I remembered incidents, moments of the past that I had completely suppressed. It was as though there was something about the passion of contact that was hypnotic, that enabled me to drop barriers and thus enter fully, rather reenter those past experiences. A key aspect seemed to be the way he smelled, the combined odors of cigarettes, occasionally alcohol, and his body smells. I thought often of the phrase "scent of memory," for it was those smells that carried me back. And there were specific occasions when it was very evident that the experience of being in his company was the catalyst for this remembering.

Two specific incidents come to mind. One day in the middle of the afternoon we met at his place. We were drinking cognac and dancing to music from the radio. He was smoking cigarettes (not only do I not smoke, but I usually make an effort to avoid smoke). As we held each other dancing those mingled odors of alcohol, sweat, and cigarettes led me to say, quite without thinking about it, "Uncle Pete." It was not that I had forgotten Uncle Pete. It was more that I had forgotten the childhood experience of meeting him. He drank often, smoked cigarettes, and always on the few occasions that we met him, he held us children in tight embraces. It was the memory of those embraces—of the way I hated and longed to resist them—that I recalled.

Another day we went to a favorite park to feed ducks and parked the car in front of tall bushes. As we were sitting there, we suddenly heard the sound of an oncoming train—a sound which startled me so that it evoked another long-suppressed memory: that of crossing the train tracks in my father's car. I recalled an incident where the car stopped on the tracks and my father left us sitting there while he raised the hood of the car and worked to repair it. This is an incident that I am not certain actually happened. As a child, I had been terrified of just such an incident occurring, perhaps so terrified that it played itself out in my mind as though it had happened. These are just two ways this encounter acted as a catalyst breaking down barriers enabling me to finally write this long-desired autobiography of my childhood.

Each day I sat at the typewriter and different memories were written about in short vignettes. They came in a rush, as though they were a sudden thunderstorm. They came in a surreal, dreamlike style which made me cease to think of them as strictly autobiographical because it seemed that myth, dream, and reality had merged. There were many incidents that I would talk about with my siblings to see if they recalled them. Often we remembered together a general outline of an incident but the details were different for us. This fact was a constant reminder of the limitations of autobiography, of the extent to which autobiography is a very personal story telling— a unique recounting of events not so much as they have happened but as we remember and invent them. One memory that I would have sworn was "the truth and nothing but the truth" concerned a wagon that my brother and I shared as a child. I remembered that we played with this toy only at my grandfather's house, that we shared it, that I would ride it and my brother would push me. Yet one facet of the memory was puzzling; I remembered always returning home with bruises or scratches from this toy. When I called my mother, she said there had never been any wagon, that we had shared a red wheelbarrow, that it had always been at my grandfather's house because there were sidewalks on that part of town. We lived in the hills where there were no sidewalks. Again I was compelled to face the fiction that is a part of all retelling, remembering. I began to think of the work I was doing as both fiction and autobiography. It seemed to fall in the category of writing that Audre Lorde, in her autobiographically based work *Zami*, calls bio-mythography. As I wrote, I felt that I was not as concerned with accuracy of detail as I was with evoking in writing the state of mind, the spirit of a particular moment.

The longing to tell one's story and the process of telling is symbolically a gesture of longing to recover the past in such a way that one experiences both a sense of reunion and a sense of release. It was the longing for release that compelled the writing but concurrently it was the joy of reunion that enabled me to see that the act of writing one's autobiography is a way to find again that aspect of self and experience that may no longer be an actual part of one's life but is a living memory shaping and informing the present. Autobiographical writing was a way for me to evoke the particular experience of growing

up southern and Black in segregated communities. It was a way
to recapture the richness of southern Black culture. The need
to remember and hold to the legacy of that experience and
what it taught me has been all the more important since I have
since lived in predominately White communities and taught
at predominately White colleges. Black southern folk experience was the foundation of the life around me when I was a
child; that experience no longer exists in many places where it
was once all of life that we knew. Capitalism, upward mobility,
assimilation of other values have all led to rapid disintegration
of Black folk experience or in some cases the gradual wearing
away of that experience.

Within the world of my childhood, we held onto the legacy
of a distinct Black culture by listening to the elders tell their
stories. Autobiography was experienced most actively in the art
of telling one's story. I can recall sitting at Baba's (my grandmother on my mother's side) at 1200 Broad Street—listening
to people come and recount their life experience. In those
days, whenever I brought a playmate to my grandmother's
house, Baba would want a brief outline of their autobiography
before we would begin playing. She wanted not only to know
who their people were but what their values were. It was sometimes an awesome and terrifying experience to stand answering
these questions or witness another playmate being subjected
to the process and yet this was the way we would come to know
our own and one another's family history. It is the absence of
such a tradition in my adult life that makes the written narrative of my girlhood all the more important. As the years pass
and these glorious memories grow much more vague, there will
remain the clarity contained within the written words.

Conceptually, the autobiography was framed in the manner
of a hope chest. I remembered my mother's hope chest, with

its wonderful odor of cedar and thought about her taking the most precious items and placing them there for safekeeping. Certain memories were for me a similar treasure. I wanted to place them somewhere for safekeeping. An autobiographical narrative seemed an appropriate place. Each particular incident, encounter, experience had its own story, sometimes told from the first person, sometimes told from the third person. Often I felt as though I was in a trance at my typewriter, that the shape of a particular memory was decided not by my conscious mind but by all that is dark and deep within me, unconscious but present. It was the act of making it present, bringing it into the open, so to speak, that was liberating.

From the perspective of trying to understand my psyche, it was also interesting to read the narrative in its entirety after I had completed the work. It had not occurred to me that bringing one's past, one's memories together in a complete narrative would allow one to view them from a different perspective, not as singular isolated events but as part of a continuum. Reading the completed manuscript, I felt as though I had an overview not so much of my childhood but of those experiences that were deeply imprinted in my consciousness. Significantly, that which was absent, left out, not included also was important. I was shocked to find at the end of my narrative that there were few incidents I recalled that involved my five sisters. Most of the incidents with siblings were with me and my brother. There was a sense of alienation from my sisters present in childhood, a sense of estrangement. This was reflected in the narrative. Another aspect of the completed manuscript that is interesting to me is the way in which the incidents describing adult men suggest that I feared them intensely, with the exception of my grandfather and a few old men. Writing the autobiographical narrative enabled me to look at my past from a different perspective and to use this knowledge as a means of self-growth and change in a practical way.

In the end I did not feel as though I had killed the Gloria of my childhood. Instead I had rescued her. She was no longer the enemy within, the little girl who had to be annihilated for the woman to come into being. In writing about her, I reclaimed that part of myself I had long ago rejected, left uncared for, just as she had often felt alone and uncared for as a child. Remembering was part of a cycle of reunion, a joining of fragments, "the bits and pieces of my heart" that the narrative made whole again.

SAPPHIRE

The Artist as Witness

patricia bell-scott

INTRODUCTION

The poet, performance artist, and novelist Sapphire was born Ramona Lofton in 1950 at Fort Ord military base in California to parents who were in the army. As a young woman, she rejected her given name, choosing the gemstone Sapphire for her personal signature. By anyone's standard, her childhood was difficult. There was sexual abuse by a father who was a soldier in World War II and the Korean War, as well as emotional and physical abandonment by a mother who had herself been battered. Despite this early trauma, Sapphire has emerged as a strong, grounded, and giving woman whose words have the power of a healing hot spring.

Previously known for her electrifying readings to progressive audiences and reviled by conservative critics for her in-your-face language, she entered the "literary mainstream" in 1996 with publication of her first novel, Push, *by Alfred A. Knopf. This novel is the story of Precious Jones, a Black illiterate, HIV-positive sixteen-year-old whose first child is the result of impregnation by her father. The world opens to her when she enrolls in a literacy class, learns to read, and begins keeping a journal. At the beginning of the novel, Precious tells the reader that "I'm gonna try to make sense and tell the truth, else what's the fucking use? Ain' enough lies and shit out there already?" Telling the truth—especially about her own life and the lives of Black women—is Sapphire's passion. In this narrative, which is derived from a 1996 interview, she describes how truth-telling fuels her writing. It is shared here with the hope that others may find inspiration and courage.*

JOURNALIZING TO WRITER

I remember starting to write in a journal in my early twenties, when I was living in the Tenderloin in San Francisco. I started out trying to record experience—never having had any validation that my life was important. For me writing is always a creative process, and everything I write is not beautiful or publishable. But *everything* starts in my journal. And most things do not start as themselves. I just write, and then within the writing a poem or story will appear.

Although I read a lot of poetry as a child, I entered into it without a lot of study. It was just something I thought I could do. Not that I did it particularly well in the beginning, or even now—but I've never had any intimidation about it. We had one of those anthologies of great American poets, and I would find the ones that I liked—the rhythmic ones—like Edgar Allan Poe.

As an adult, I was introduced to poetry through watching Ntozake Shange experiment with choreography and poetry. This was before publication of the now famous choreopoem *for colored girls who have considered suicide/when the rainbow is enuf.* I took classes from Raymond Sawyer, and she danced and read poetry with his dance company. Here I saw poetry as performance. I didn't think of it as anything else.

By the 1980s when I came to New York, my primary influence was Alice Walker. I don't know at exactly what point I read *The Third Life of Grange Copeland,* but this book shifted my world. I had never read anything dealing with battering. So it changed me.

Although I had been writing for some time, I was almost forty before I claimed my identity as a writer. In 1990, when I did my last major performance, a fifty-minute choreopoem, "Are You Ready to Rock," my business manager, a wonderful young African American woman, said to me, "If I'm going to promote you as a writer, where's the writing? Where's the book?" I was trying to do the performance work, trying to write, and none of it was making a living. I was exhausted. Dead tired. And I couldn't go on.

I went through an intense midlife-turning-forty crisis. I felt that I had not really done much with my life, when I compared myself to my mentors like Ntozake, who had five to six books. Then I looked at some of the reasons I hadn't tried. A lack of confidence—a belief that maybe I couldn't do it or that I wasn't good or smart enough. I also realized that I had never committed myself to any one thing. I had always tried to dance, act, and write at the same time.

With this awareness, I decided to totally commit myself to becoming a writer. I said, "I will put together a collection of writings for publication," and that became *American Dreams.* I said, "I will go to school and get an MFA degree"; and I did.

These outward things gave me a sense of purpose. I was already doing the inner things—like writing every day. If writing made you a writer, I was already one. But without some outward validation like a book, you don't feel like a writer. After this crisis, the universe started to affirm me. When my poem "Rabbit-Man" won a contest, it was like God saying, "Yes, this is the right thing for you to do."

WRITING SELF-VISIBILITY

Some people call my early poems confessional. For me it has always been about erasing a certain kind of invisibility, about saying that someone like me exists. I was a young Black woman born on an army base, working as a go-go dancer in New York City, and bisexual. I had never been nor ever really intended to be married and didn't have any children. Was politically conscious but at the same time couldn't comfortably join the Black Panthers or the Nation of Islam based on what they said about gay people. Was also somewhat closer to the street than the Black academics. There were no first-person poems by a Black woman like me—someone who had been involved in the sex industry, someone who was expressing ambivalence about sexuality.

All this and more comes through in my poetry. I wasn't writing, "We're just so happy to be lesbian. We've found a new land and there's no conflict." I wasn't denying my sexuality. I was questioning it and trying to place it in context. I asked myself, "How can I talk about nationhood, and I'm out here go-go dancing? How can I talk about radical lesbian feminist separatism, and I slept with a man last night?" I was aware of my own contradictions and writing about them. As I have moved forward with my writing, I think of it as witnessing and testimony.

CHOOSING WORDS

I would choose the word "radical" to describe my work if it means challenging the status quo. I also accept the word "angry" because a lot of my writing—definitely "Wild Thing" and "Strange Juice (Or the murder of Latasha Harlins)"— expresses anger. Even some of the quieter poems—"in my father's house," "Rabbit-Man," and "One Day"—express a kind of anger. Not a ferocious anger, but a *useful* anger. It's the anger of a mature person who sees what denial and abuse rob from people.

I am definitely about women's rights and eradicating the oppression of women. So in that way I identify as a feminist. However, I have difficulty with the word sometimes because it catapults you into what is seen as a very White arena. But I don't back down from words, and I don't reject the feminist label. I'm also a bisexual who identifies as a lesbian just because that word seems to wreak terror in people's hearts. And I identify as an African American—although we are a multi-racial people—because that's the word that got us here.

More than anything, I identify as a Black person and as a woman. These are the constants. Other things change. I've watched myself go from heterosexual to lesbian to bisexual. And I've watched myself go from $5,000 a year to money. Now I'm watching myself go from young to middle-aged to one day I'll be old. But I will *always* be Black and female. No matter how much money I have, I still can't get a cab in New York City. No matter how articulate I am or how many degrees I get, I can't run through Central Park without fear of being raped. These things do not go away.

I've gotten overwhelming support for my work. I believe people turn out for me knowing that I get attacked by conservatives and that I don't always get support. I've had many Black women say, "Thank you. You've told our story. You've filled a vacuum." They've let me know that my work has made a real difference in their lives.

Many Black men have also been supportive. I will never forget the reaction of the man at the shop who copied my book manuscript. He was a regular brother with muscles, a T-shirt sizes too small, and gold chains. He seemed to be taking his time, and I was getting mad—until he turned to me with tears in his eyes and asked, "Lady, did you write this here literature?" I said, "Yes I did." Then he said, "This is some powerful literature." He had been standing there with his back to me, reading the book as he copied it.

There are also those who are embarrassed by my work. One Black woman radio talk show host told me that she had never heard of anyone like Precious. She said that I was a tool of White people and that the only reason *Push* was being heavily promoted was that it presented a dysfunctional view of the Black family. I asked if she had read the recent newspaper story about two Black women sentenced to life imprisonment for the murder of their daughters. The murder had included penetration of one child's vagina with a hairbrush. The host said that she had heard about that but that *those* people were on drugs. In other words, despite the newspaper story my work was still false.

To people like these—folks in denial—my work is offensive. I counter the idea that racism is the only thing affecting us and that if it would just go away, we would have a happy life. Racism may create the emotional climate that allows child abuse to happen, but it wasn't the Ku Klux Klan who came in there and killed those baby girls.

THE ARTIST DENIED

Because I put myself out there by identifying some of the work in the first person, I'm often not seen as a writer. I'm seen as the homosexual, the ex-prostitute, the incest survivor—the thing as opposed to the artist. One time an associate called to tell me that a well-known Black woman writer wanted to talk to me. I was excited and flattered—until I learned that she wanted to talk to a prostitute. I was devastated. I had loved this woman's book so much. I told the intermediary that I was busy and couldn't meet with her.

I was also denied the opportunity to be in one of the first mainstream gay and lesbian anthologies. When the editors contacted me about including "New York City Tonight," a poem about prostitution, I told them that this had been published over and over again and that I wanted to present myself in a different vein. But they wouldn't take any other work. So I ended up not being in that anthology. I felt that they were trying to discredit my artistry. This kind of thing has happened to me a lot, and it is frustrating. And you know people didn't do this to Anne Sexton—even though she talked about being in a nuthouse! They didn't say to her, "Oh, it is so wonderful to have a mental patient here with us today." And they didn't go up to Ernest Hemingway and say, "Oh, how wonderful that we have an alcoholic here with us today." They wouldn't dream of doing anything like that to them. But people have no problem doing that to me.

WRITING A DAUGHTER

Before *Push,* I knew that I was going to write a book based on literacy and Harlem in the nineties. Once I started writing, Precious just came to me. In the beginning, I wrote from a distance—on the outside of her. Later I totally entered her, so much so that I could feel her sweating. I've never had such an experience of character. I felt like I was pregnant, like she was coming out through my pen, like I had had a beautiful child. I think of it now as deep listening.

Precious is a totally fictional character, although I have known several young women with her experience. I remember the day that one of my literacy ed students—a thirty-two-year-old ex-addict, very beautiful and articulate—mentioned that she was having trouble getting a baby-sitter. When she said that the oldest child was twenty, I probably stared. So she explained that she had had this child by her father when she was twelve and that that baby was born with Down's syndrome. Another time a different student got up to leave class early. And I told her that she couldn't leave, that class was not over until such and such a time, and that she had a commitment. Well, she looked at me like the fool I was and said in front of the whole class, "Miss Sapphire, I have to pick up my son from the baby-sitter and I'm having trouble getting my

AZT." Stories like this stayed with me and helped me envision the fictional characters I created in *Push*.

WRITING TO TRANSFORM

I see *Push* as a healing novel and a story of triumph. The writing, however, wasn't particularly healing for me. Here I created homelessness, HIV, and this horrible mother and father. Instead of it being a past memory that released me, I lived with tension and pain. I tried to show that a profound alteration in this child's consciousness could allow her to love herself and her son. If there is anything to learn from this novel, it's that Precious is a valuable human being.

Of the characters in this novel who are represented out there in the world, Precious is the one who has no picture in people's minds. When I was writing, welfare had not been abolished. It was up for grabs, and now they're forcing teenage mothers to go back to their own mothers. Can you imagine Precious going back to live at Mama's house? People wouldn't suggest this if they could see the faces of the girls they were talking about. Some of them have been abused in the home, and many of them have been abandoned. In my mind, abandonment may be worse than abuse. Most kids live through abuse, but if you just put them in a trash can, they die.

The more I live, the more I understand that people are brought into the world for different reasons. Some are brought to have the perfect child, some to have the perfect relationship, or for other reasons. I know that this writing is what I was brought here to do. And my purpose is to get out the word, to witness, and give testimony. So I'm on a mission—*definitely* on a mission.

HARRIET ANN BUCKLEY

An Artist Storyteller

juanita johnson-bailey

INTRODUCTION

*"Resonating my African ancestry I make spirit/message objects,"
says Harriet Ann Buckley. Inspired by such artists as Mary Greer
and David Green, she draws herself and her communities. Formally
educated as a painter and graduated from the Memphis College of
Art, she works in the medium demanded by the subject. Her art
often appears three-dimensional, combining quilting, photography,
painting, leather, and metal to create unique forms. She is most
prolific in watercolors, although she strives to learn innovative
techniques so that new images can emerge. [One of her watercolors,
"Keepers of the Culture," is featured on the cover of this book.] Her
colors communicate an Afro-Caribbean palette, celebrating scenes
as familiar as hair rituals and as unnerving as genital mutilation.*

*Harriet sketches constantly throughout the day, filling jour-
nal after journal with the private language of art. She does not*

want to "miss a thing." At her home, in the midst of quilts, oil paintings, sketchbook journals, ancestral boxes and drums, larger-than-life papier-mâché sculptures, and watercolors, a wire sculpture jumps out. It is a woman's head with jeweled-fire eyes, leather-worked facial features, and a mass of color-beaded dreadlocks. She calls it "Dreaded Me" and explains that it refers sometimes to her dreadlocks and at other times to her persona.

In a pursuit that began when she started drawing as a child, Harriet is a nonconformist. Initially her fervor was to draw pictures that looked like her. Later she sought to communicate her people's struggle and scenes of injustice. Now she feels that her work has evolved into a narrative art that speaks beyond her personal experience and addresses the Black woman collectively. Harriet's art is a survival lifeline that reveals, interprets, and confirms the existence of Black women—most especially to Black women.

ART IS MY PERSONAL LANGUAGE

All of my art is stories, and I've been criticized for always telling stories. But it is important to tell before the story is changed, corrupted, or Xed out completely. So I am constantly narrating stories in my artwork.

As an artist I am always telling the story of my people, and I carry a journal with me to record when something special hits me. I don't write in my journal; I sketch in it so I can capture memories for my subconscious to bring out later. I constantly start and stop in my journals. It is as if something tells me to put one away for later and move on to another journal. I've been sketching in one on and off since 1984. This is my language, and I'm reading when I look at my sketched journal entries.

I have piles of journals dating back to the 1980s. There are so many different sizes. Some fit in my pocket, and others I carry in my arms. The large ones are my main journals. Some I buy, and many I make putting buttons or bells on them for privacy and safekeeping. This is my means of having a lock and key on my personal thoughts.

Every journal entry is from a life event—either things that happened to me or things that I am stimulated to imagine. At times an account may be complete unto itself, and at other times my drawings might form a series. The older I get, the more my intuition opens up and the more my language evolves. Having no control over it, I find that concepts come into my mind at will and I dutifully record them. Even things I don't remember seem to be stories in my mind's house just waiting to come to the page. Strangely enough, my subconscious knows what to do. It puts the language together, making the wax and watercolor merge into form and shape.

It's the responsibility of the artist to record her own language and to leave clues so that somebody can read and interpret. That's one reason why I can't go totally abstract. Without reference points how can people know what I was intending? While I think trees are feminine and always paint them with the roots showing, if I don't explain that now, someone might think I was doing a root study. Although I do appreciate the value of abstract, I seldom use it to communicate. As a Black woman I have things to say and must say them directly or I will burst.

I am busy telling the truth—that we exist, that we are strong, flexible, and intelligent. I am seeing and I am letting people see things that they need to see and won't.

DRAWING MY ABCS

I remember drawing in first grade. My little tablets had more drawings than lessons in them. My mother, who was a first-grade teacher, also drew. I was always drawing, cutting things out, and painting, and as I improved I started doing bulletin boards for the other teachers. I can't remember not drawing after that early beginning.

In high school I loved art a lot and made up reasons to get excused from other classes just so I could spend extra time in the art classroom. The earliest pieces in my collection come from my high school art classes. This was also the first time I did anything on canvas board. I did an oil pastel Madonna piece that I gave to my father's aunt as a present. It was a good feeling. The faces were Black. Even at that point I had to see me in my work.

When I went to art school, it was the first time I'd ever gone to school with White kids. This was quite an eye-opener because I was the only person of color in my classes. All of the instructors were White. I'd ask, "Don't you know any Black artists to talk about in the lessons?" They didn't. I'd find examples and tell my teachers about them. I wanted to know someone like me. Only one Black artist came as a visiting lecturer the entire time I was in college.

Teachers were constantly trying to mold me in the image of all the other students. At every turn they were telling me, "Your images are not right." The low grades on my notebooks reflected their opinions of my work, which was totally different from everybody else's. In big letters written back to me were, "Where did this come from? These do not fit!" I would get Cs and someone who turned in a late assignment with far less work in it than mine would get an A. That hit me. I knew something was wrong.

By my senior year I had written my thesis and had created a body of work. I had gone from the regular format of squares and rectangles to puzzlelike pieces. Occasionally they were rounded, and my canvases were shaped differently because we [Blacks] don't fit into the same pegs. Teachers were amazed and decided I was a universalist. When one of the students asked, "How do you think your work is universal?" I said, "I'm universal, so my work is universal."

NURTURED BY MANY COMMUNITIES

When I produce art now it is like birthing. My pieces are like my children. They are parts of me. My art is evolving because at forty-eight I am in another place, existing in many communities. As a Black woman I'm first of all in that community with my race. Next I am in a community of women of color. Then I look in the mirror and see being in love with another woman as setting me in another community. I'm in lots of communities, and I need all of them to exist.

My work centers on women because it centers on me and because there are not enough good visual images of Black women. I've noticed that when I do workshops with our kids they don't even take out the brown color to paint faces. They draw our faces and leave them the color of the paper. If the paper happens to be white, that's it. If the paper is colored, well, it might stay that way. Whenever I have images of myself I try to make them various shades of brown to make a statement.

I find myself doing more work about us as women, which is I guess the normal progression. Many of the women and scenes that I encountered on a recent trip to St. Croix can be seen in my work. The first night on the island I met a women's percussion group called Keepers of the Culture. They were the first women of color percussion group I had ever seen, and I was fascinated by them. They became integral to my time and work on the island, especially when we started our celebration dances. This came about because my partner, a dancer, wanted to dance. So we located a woman dance teacher, formed dance meetings, and Keepers of the Culture would drum. Every Wednesday night the drummers would convene and women would come out of the bush—walking long distances—to dance. The instructor was a large woman who floated when she moved. She danced everyone to exhaustion. For months it was just madness, healing madness. I drew women's bodies in movement as they danced and found myself beating on my sketchbook. I ended up drumming and making my own drums as art, incorporating cowrie shells, bells, my dreadlocks, and pieces of my partner's dance outfits into my drums.

I met Audre Lorde, who is probably the most recent influence on my work, during this trip to St. Croix. I had read her books but had never met her. When I saw her, I actually didn't know who she was. She sat in front of me at a Sweet Honey in the Rock concert, and people were coming from everywhere to pay homage. I said to myself, "I don't know who she is, but this is a queen here." Two days later I found out. Meeting her was a turning point. She helped me to see that excluding any part of myself from my work or being afraid to show all aspects was in a sense saying that certain parts are not acceptable. Now I don't let people have the option of telling me this should be a little more orange or green to go with my sofa. I don't get motivated to paint pictures to go with sofas. I'm not a house painter—been there, done that. I've learned to put all of the work out there. That is what Audre Lorde taught me.

As my work has become more woman centered I have been criticized. One White male artist looked at my sketchbook and said, "You must be a feminist. You have nothing but women in your book." I asked, "So if you had a book with women in it, would that make you a feminist?" There was silence.

I am not a person who can fit in a little box. I graduated with a painting degree but can't be labeled as a painter. I belong to a craft group but am not really a craftsperson. I used to belong to a photography group, but I didn't just do photography. Each new technique allows subconscious images to leap out. It is as if images had been hindered because I did not have the mode of expression at my fingertips. A new medium allows my head, my heart, my feelings, and skills to become one. It makes me more fluid.

I incorporate painting on fabric and gourds. I carve and paint on leather, create papier-mâché-and-wire sculptures, quilt, and paint and draw with oils, watercolors, markers, and wax. I want to experiment with everything.

This new body of work on women is taking me places. I can be in public and see clothed bodies that speak to me. I've just completed a collection of female nudes. One day the figure of this woman who was riding the bus just hit me. Thank God I had my journal. I had to draw her. I have started concentrating on our various body types as my body has started to change, leaving them without clothes so you can see and appreciate other shapes.

MY INSIDER'S PERSPECTIVE

One of the enduring criticisms of my work is that it is "too Black." And I say I am not White. What am I supposed to do here? You are supposed to create things in your own environment. Paint where you come from. Now if I painted as if I were from a White environment, the audience would be angry and totally critical. I can express only my life's interactions. I don't get what they're saying, "Your work is too Black." I'd like to know, "What is too Black?" I'd like to know this concept. How can you get too Black? Black is a good thing, and my work says that I am a Black woman artist.

I have been rejected so many times, it is disheartening. It can get tiresome. But I create what I know. There's no other way to come from, at least for me.

My paintings have been taken off the walls after I'd left them for a show. I remember once being so enraged that I demanded they give me my painting. I left walking, carrying it with me as the police followed. I guess they thought I was stealing it, so they followed me home. Now every time I'm asked to exhibit at a show I ask first, "What kind of show is this? Are there restrictions? Is my painting coming off the wall? Are there any guidelines?" I've shown in some unusual places in order to have my work seen. I have presented in the park, hanging paintings between trees.

Living off your art can be very difficult. There have been moments in my life of no lights, no gas, water, food, or car. Art is life. It is my heartbeat. It's the blood rushing through my body.

DEPICTING OUR CULTURE

Working on subjects that center Black women comes naturally. Right now I am doing a series on hair. It has been a study of mine because of my childhood. My mother started taking me to the beauty salon when I was so small that the lady [beautician] had to sit me in a chair on top of telephone books in order for me to get my hair washed, dried, and fried. It was persecution because my mom would leave me there and the lady would not wait on me until my mom came back. This meant that I would be at the beauty shop all day.

I've gone through the Afro, close-cropped hair, and now dreadlocks. My grandmothers were living when I first wore an Afro. They thought it was the most hideous thing to do because my hair was already kinky and their desire was to straighten it. When I started dreading, people asked, "Why must you wear your hair like that?" When I do workshops for children the first question out of their mouths is, "Is that your hair?" I can understand why. You can put many things on your head and call it hair. Hair is so political to us as a race. I've started doing watercolors about that.

I am thinking of doing a body of work around menopause. I'm going through the change, and since my mom has been deceased for twenty years, I didn't hear any conversations about the change. The cycle controls so much of our body, and women don't talk about it enough, especially from one generation to the next. The flashes are incredible, and I've been searching for an image that really expresses it. Because of the flow, watercolors may be best.

Now I am reflecting on the entire process of the woman's life cycle. I started thinking on it when I did a quilt after reading Alice Walker's *Possessing the Secret of Joy*, about how some women and girls do not enjoy their sexuality and sex because their genitalia are destroyed. Two of my journals are full of images that came after I read this book. I've also done a quilt about genital mutilation. It contains the Ghanian Akan symbol, *nkonsondonson*, which means we are linked together in life and death. I often use symbols in my art because they are more powerful than words. In this quilt I wove Alice Walker's image of the chicken figure, the elder woman who performs the mutilation, her instruments, and the body of the young girl being damaged. I surrounded all this by the knees of the little girls who will be hurt in the future holding down the present-day victim. And at the bottom of the quilt, I stitched in a tree of hope—strong and flexible. The Akan symbol, *sankofa,* is also there. It means mistakes can always be undone. In other words, we can undo this mess and stop this torture. In the background there is a young woman watching it all. I have no idea where she came from, but she insisted on being part of this piece of art. I guess one of the ancestors came to look.

When I am making pieces like this quilt, I know that I am part of a cycle that includes the ancestors and those who are yet to come. Producing art helps me leave behind a legacy of images. I have noticed that when ancient civilizations cease to exist it is the art that lives. And I'm proud to say that some of this will still be here when I'm gone—in some form or another. I like that. This famous artist always asks me, "Are you still doing art?" I respond, "Is the air still blowing out here? Is that tree still green?"

AUTOBIOGRAPHY

(for my mother)

marita golden

she was a heroine
in the grand tradition
of heroines who
imprisoned by the commonplace
scale the walls
defy barking dogs mobilized to
retrieve
too fast for search light's tango
puzzled and luminous against a
mute uncooperative sky
never once captured
yet always there
in the morning
behind bars
self governed
savoring a victory the warden
will never see

there were three husbands
one small fortune
two children
five houses
cars and the kind of clothes
she promised herself at sixteen
one day to have
unexpected, i filled her womb
at forty-two
at fifty six she told me
"anything that was ever any good for me
arrived as a total surprise."

men found her a fire
to restore them
warm and grateful, always
they tried to put her out

finally alone
with nothing left to prove
the rest unabridged, inescapable
she said
"i like me with no
interruptions/mergers
no one but me to fulfill
or dissect."

she said
she was happy

and i believe she was.

PART II

CLAIMING LIVES LOST

And where the words of women are crying to be heard, we must each of us recognize our responsibility to seek those words out, to read them and share them and examine them in their pertinence to our lives.

—AUDRE LORDE

I Sell the Shadow to Support the Substance.

SOJOURNER TRUTH.

I Sell the Shadow to Support the Substance (1864), Sojourner Truth. Sojourner Truth, former slave, preacher, lecturer, abolitionist, and feminist, chose this *carte de visite* as her favorite portrait just as she chose her name "Truth" in an attempt to shape and direct her life story. Her clothing, posture, knitting, and open book connote a breeding and social class status decidedly different from the image of Truth as an unsophisticated slave woman. Photographer unidentified, © National Portrait Gallery, Smithsonian Institution.

THROUGH THE STORM, THROUGH THE NIGHT

brenda faye bell

Our Father, who are in heaven,
I'm coming home. No alternative.
Shelters packed. Halfway-house
half-way cross town. No buses running.
I'd go back to Wanda's but she's gone back to Will
and he's gone back to Wyoming. Yeah, Wyoming.
Got myself thrown in jail
but the judge—in the spirit of Christmas—
turned me loose. So I'm coming home to you.

Lead me, Guide me, through the snow and over the ice.
Don't wanna get lost on this highway to heaven.
Haven't ventured your way since I was a little girl
walking down the aisle to get baptized.
Yeah, you know me Lord,
Hell is much closer to my stomping ground.

And I know you've forgiven me
seventy times seven times seventy more.
And here I am begging for yet another pardon.
But it's been that kind of day—
when begging ain't brought me nothing.
No bed. No blanket. No bottle. Even in a blizzard!

Lead me, Guide me through the snow, over the ice.
Lead me on to the light. Precious Lord, take my hand.

The storm is
passing over
Hallelu

LOOKING FOR ZORA

alice walker

On January 16, 1959, Zora Neale Hurston, suffering from the effects of a stroke and writing painfully in longhand, composed a letter to the "editorial department" of Harper & Brothers inquiring if they would be interested in seeing "the book I am laboring upon at present—a life of Herod the Great." One year and twelve days later, Zora Neale Hurston died without funds to provide for her burial, a resident of the St. Lucie County, Florida, Welfare Home. She lies today in an unmarked grave in a segregated cemetery in Fort Pierce, Florida, a resting place generally symbolic of the Black writer's fate in America.

Zora Neale Hurston is one of the most significant unread authors in America, the author of two minor classics and four other major books.

> —*Robert Hemenway,*
> *"Zora Hurston and the Eatonville Anthropology,"*
> The Harlem Renaissance Remembered

On August 15, 1973, I wake up just as the plane is lowering over Sanford, Florida, which means I am also looking down on Eatonville, Zora Neale Hurston's birthplace. I recognize it from Zora's description in *Mules and Men:* "the city of five lakes, three croquet courts, three hundred brown skins, three hundred good swimmers, plenty guavas, two schools, and no jailhouse." Of course I cannot see the guavas, but the five lakes are still there, and it is the lakes I count as the plane prepares to land in Orlando.

From the air, Florida looks completely flat, and as we near the ground this impression does not change. This is the first time I have seen the interior of the state, which Zora wrote about so well, but there are the acres of orange groves, the sand, mangrove trees, and scrub pine that I know from her books. Getting off the plane I walk through the humid air of midday into the tacky but air-conditioned airport. I search for Charlotte Hunt, my companion on the Zora Hurston expedition. She lives in Winter Park, Florida, very near Eatonville, and is writing her graduate dissertation on Zora. I see her waving—a large, pleasant-faced White woman in dark glasses. We have written to each other for several weeks, swapping our latest finds (mostly hers) on Zora, and trying to make sense out of the mass of information obtained (often erroneous or simply confusing) from Zora herself—through her stories and autobiography—and from people who wrote about her.

Eatonville has lived for such a long time in my imagination that I can hardly believe it will be found existing in its own right. But after twenty minutes on the expressway, Charlotte turns off and I see a small settlement of houses and stores set with no particular pattern in the sandy soil off the road. We stop in front of a neat gray building that has two fascinating signs: EATONVILLE POST OFFICE and EATONVILLE CITY HALL.

Inside the Eatonville City Hall half of the building, a slender, dark-brown–skinned woman sits looking through letters on a desk. When she hears we are searching for anyone who might have known Zora Neale Hurston, she leans back in thought. Because I don't wish to inspire foot-dragging in people who might know something about Zora they're not sure they should tell, I have decided on a simple, but I feel profoundly *useful*, lie.

"I am Miss Hurston's niece," I prompt the young woman, who brings her head down with a smile.

"I think Mrs. Moseley is about the only one still living who might remember her," she says.

"Do you mean *Mathilda* Moseley, the woman who tells those 'woman is smarter than man' lies in Zora's book?"

"Yes," says the young woman. "Mrs. Moseley is real old now, of course. But this time of day, she should be at home."

I stand at the counter looking down on her, the first Eatonville resident I have spoken to. Because of Zora's books, I feel I know something about her; at least I know what the town she grew up in was like years before she was born.

"Tell me something," I say. "Do the schools teach Zora's books here?"

"No," she says, "they don't. I don't think most people know anything about Zora Neale Hurston, or know about any of the great things she did. She was a fine lady. I've read all of her books myself, but I don't think many other folks in Eatonville have."

"Many of the church people around here, as I understand it," says Charlotte in a murmured aside, "thought Zora was pretty loose. I don't think they appreciated her writing about them."

"Well," I say to the young woman, "thank you for your help." She clarifies her directions to Mrs. Moseley's house and smiles as Charlotte and I turn to go.

The letter to Harper's does not expose a publisher's rejection of an unknown masterpiece, but it does reveal how the bright promise of the Harlem Renaissance deteriorated for many of the writers who shared in its exuberance. It also indicates the personal tragedy of Zora Neale Hurston: Barnard graduate, author of four novels, two books of folklore, one volume of autobiography, the most important collector of Afro-American folklore in America, reduced by poverty and circumstance to seek a publisher by unsolicited mail.

—*Robert Hemenway*

Zora Hurston was born in 1901, 1902, or 1903—depending on how old she felt herself to be at the time someone asked.

—*Librarian, Beinecke Library, Yale University*

The Moseley house is small and white and snug, its tiny yard nearly swallowed up by oleanders and hibiscus bushes. Charlotte and I knock on the door. I call out. But there is no answer. This strikes us as peculiar. We have had time to figure out an age for Mrs. Moseley—not dates or a number, just old. I am thinking of a quivery, bedridden invalid when we hear the car. We look behind us to see an old black-and-white Buick—paint peeling and grillwork rusty—pulling into the drive. A neat old lady in a purple dress and with white hair is straining at the wheel. She is frowning because Charlotte's car is in the way.

Mrs. Moseley looks at us suspiciously. "Yes, I knew Zora Neale," she says, unsmilingly and with a rather cold stare at Charlotte (who, I imagine, feels very *White* at that moment), "but that was a long time ago, and I don't want to talk about it."

"Yes, ma'am," I murmur, bringing all my sympathy to bear on the situation.

"Not only that," Mrs. Moseley continues, "I've been sick. Been in the hospital for an operation. Ruptured artery. The doctors didn't believe I was going to live, but you see me alive, don't you?"

"Looking well, too," I comment.

Mrs. Moseley is out of her car. A thin, sprightly woman with nice gold-studded false teeth, uppers and lowers. I like her because she stands there *straight* beside her car, with a hand on her hip and her straw pocketbook on her arm. She wears white T-strap shoes with heels that show off her well-shaped legs.

"I'm eighty-two years old, you know," she says. "And I just can't remember things the way I used to. Anyhow, Zora Neale left here to go to school and she never really came back to live. She'd come here for material for her books, but that was all. She spent most of her time down in South Florida."

"You know, Mrs. Moseley, I saw your name in one of Zora's books."

"You did?" She looks at me with only slightly more interest. "I read some of her books a long time ago, but then people got to borrowing and borrowing and they borrowed them all away."

"I could send you a copy of everything that's been reprinted," I offer. "Would you like me to do that?"

"No," says Mrs. Moseley promptly. "I don't read much any more. Besides, all of that was so long ago. . . ."

Charlotte and I settle back against the car in the sun. Mrs. Moseley tells us at length and with exact recall every step in her recent operation, ending with: "What those doctors didn't know—when they were expecting me to die (and they didn't even think I'd live long enough for them to have to take out my stitches!)—is that Jesus is the best doctor, and if *He* says for you to get well, that's all that counts."

With this philosophy, Charlotte and I murmur quick assent: being Southerners and church bred, we have heard that belief before. But what we learn from Mrs. Moseley is that she does not remember much beyond the year 1938. She shows us a picture of her father and mother and says that her father was Joe Clarke's brother. Joe Clarke, as every Zora Hurston reader knows, was the first mayor of Eatonville; his fictional counterpart is Jody Starks of *Their Eyes Were Watching God*. We also get directions to where Joe Clarke's store *was*—where Club Eaton is now. Club Eaton, a long orange-beige nightspot we had seen on the main road, is apparently famous for the good times in it regularly had by all. It is, perhaps, the modern equivalent of the store porch, where all the men of Zora's childhood came to tell "lies," that is, Black folk tales, that were "made and used on the spot," to take a line from Zora. As for Zora's exact birthplace, Mrs. Moseley has no idea.

After I have commented on the healthy growth of her hibiscus bushes, she becomes more talkative. She mentions how much she *loved* to dance, when she was a young woman, and talks about how good her husband was. When he was alive, she says, she was completely happy because he allowed her to be completely free. "I was so free I had to pinch myself sometimes to tell if I was a married woman."

Relaxed now, she tells us about going to school with Zora. "Zora and I went to the same school. It's called Hungerford High now. It *was* only to the eighth grade. But our teachers were so good that by the time you left you knew college subjects. When I went to Morris Brown in Atlanta, the teachers there were just teaching me the same things I had already learned right in Eatonville. I wrote Mama and told her I was going to come home and help her with her babies. I wasn't learning anything new."

"Tell me something, Mrs. Moseley," I ask. "Why do you suppose Zora was against integration? I read somewhere that she was against school desegregation because she felt it was an insult to Black teachers."

"Oh, one of them [White people] came around asking me about integration. One day I was doing my shopping. I heard 'em over there talking about it in the store, about the schools. And I got on out of the way because I knew if they asked me, they wouldn't like what I was going to tell 'em. But they came up and asked me anyhow. 'What do you think about this integration?' one of them said. I acted like I thought I had heard wrong. 'You're asking *me* what *I* think about integration?' I said. 'Well, as you can see, I'm just an old colored woman'—I was seventy-five or seventy-six then—'and this is the first time anybody ever asked me about integration. And nobody asked my grandmother what she thought, either, but her daddy was one of you all.' " Mrs. Moseley seems satisfied with this memory of her rejoinder. She looks at Charlotte. "I have the blood of three races in my veins," she says belligerently, "White, Black, and Indian, and nobody asked me *anything* before."

"Do you think living in Eatonville made integration less appealing to you?"

"Well, I can tell you this: I have lived in Eatonville all my life, and I've been in the governing of this town. I've been everything but mayor and I've been *assistant* mayor. Eatonville was and is an all-Black town. We have our own police department, post office, and town hall. Our own school and good teachers. Do I need integration?

"They took over Goldsboro, because the Black people who lived there never incorporated, like we did. And now I don't even know if any Black folks live there. They built big houses up there around the lakes. But we didn't let that happen in Eatonville, and we don't sell land to just anybody. And you see, we're still here."

When we leave, Mrs. Moseley is standing by her car, waving. I think of the letter Roy Wilkins wrote to a Black newspaper blasting Zora Neale for her lack of enthusiasm about the integration of schools. I wonder if he knew the experience of Eatonville she was coming from. Not many Black people in America have come from a self-contained, all-Black community where loyalty and unity are taken for granted. A place where Black pride is nothing new.

There is, however, one thing Mrs. Moseley said that bothered me.

"Tell me, Mrs. Moseley," I had asked, "why is it that thirteen years after Zora's death, no marker has been put on her grave?"

And Mrs. Moseley answered: "The reason she doesn't have a stone is because she wasn't buried here. She was buried down in South Florida somewhere. I don't think anybody really knew where she was."

Only to reach a wider audience, need she ever write books—because she is a perfect book of entertainment in herself. In her youth she was always getting scholarships and things from wealthy White people, some of whom simply paid her just to sit around and represent the Negro race for them, she did it in such a racy fashion. She was full of sidesplitting anecdotes, humorous tales, and tragicomic stories, remembered out of her life in the South as a daughter of a traveling minister of God. She could make you laugh one minute and cry the next. To many of her White friends, no doubt, she was a perfect "darkie," in the nice meaning they give the term—that is, a naive, childlike, sweet, humorous, and highly colored Negro.

But Miss Hurston was clever, too—a student who didn't let college give her a broad "a" and who had great scorn for all pretensions, academic or otherwise. That is why she was such a fine folklore collector, able to go among the people and never act as if she had been to school at all. Almost nobody else could stop the average Harlemite on Lenox Avenue and measure his head with a strange-looking, anthropological device and not get bawled out for the attempt, except Zora, who used to stop anyone whose head looked interesting, and measure it.

—*Langston Hughes,* The Big Sea

What does it matter what White folks must have thought about her?

—*Student, Black women writers class, Wellesley College*

Mrs. Sarah Peek Patterson is a handsome, red-haired woman in her late forties, wearing orange slacks and gold earrings. She is the director of Lee-Peek Mortuary in Fort Pierce, the establishment that handled Zora's burial. Unlike most Black funeral homes in southern towns that sit like palaces among the general poverty, Lee-Peek has a run-down, *small* look. Perhaps this is because it is painted purple and white, as are its Cadillac chariots. These colors do not age well. The rooms are cluttered and grimy, and the bathroom is a tiny, stale-smelling prison, with a bottle of black hair dye (apparently used to touch up the hair of the corpses) dripping into the face bowl. Two pine burial boxes are resting in the bathtub.

Mrs. Patterson herself is pleasant and helpful.

"As I told you over the phone, Mrs. Patterson," I begin, shaking her hand and looking into her penny-brown eyes, "I am Zora Neale Hurston's niece, and I would like to have a marker put on her grave. You said, when I called you last week, that you could tell me where the grave is."

By this time I am, of course, completely into being Zora's niece, and the lie comes with perfect naturalness to my lips. Besides, as far as I'm concerned, she *is* my aunt—and that of all Black people as well.

"She was buried in 1960," exclaims Mrs. Patterson. "That was when my father was running this funeral home. He's sick now or I'd let you talk to him. But I know where she's buried. She's in the old cemetery, the Garden of the Heavenly Rest, on Seventeenth Street. Just when you go in the gate there's a circle, and she's buried right in the middle of it. Hers is the only grave in that circle—because people don't bury in that cemetery any more."

She turns to a stocky, black-skinned woman in her thirties, wearing a green polo shirt and white jeans cut off at the knee. "This lady will show you where it is," she says.

"I can't tell you how much I appreciate this," I say to Mrs. Patterson, as I rise to go. "And could you tell me something else? You see, I never met my aunt. When she died, I was still a junior in high school. But could you tell me what she died of, and what kind of funeral she had?"

"I don't know exactly what she died of," Mrs. Patterson says. "I know she didn't have any money. Folks took up a collection to bury her. . . . I believe she died of malnutrition."

"*Malnutrition?*"

Outside, in the blistering sun, I lean my head against Charlotte's even more blistering car top. The sting of the hot metal only intensifies my anger. *"Malnutrition,"* I manage to mutter. "Hell, our condition hasn't changed *any* since Phillis Wheatley's time. *She* died of malnutrition!"

"Really?" says Charlotte. "I didn't know that."

One cannot overemphasize the extent of her commitment. It was so great that her marriage in the spring of 1927 to Herbert Sheen was short-lived. Although divorce did not come officially until 1931, the two separated amicably after only a few months, Hurston to continue her collecting, Sheen to attend Medical School. Hurston never married again.

—*Robert Hemenway*

"What is your name?" I ask the woman who has climbed into the backseat.

"Rosalee," she says. She has a rough, pleasant voice, as if she is a singer who also smokes a lot. She is homely, and has an air of ready indifference.

"Another woman came by here wanting to see the grave," she says, lighting up a cigarette. "She was a little short, dumpty White lady from one of these Florida schools. Orlando or Daytona. But let me tell you something before we gets started. All I know is where the cemetery is. I don't know one thing about that grave. You better go back in and ask her to draw you a map."

A few moments later, with Mrs. Patterson's diagram of where the grave is, we head for the cemetery.

We drive past blocks of small, pastel-colored houses and turn right onto Seventeenth Street. At the very end, we reach a tall curving gate, with the words "Garden of the Heavenly Rest" fading into the stone. I expected, from Mrs. Patterson's small drawing, to find a small circle—which would have placed Zora's grave five or ten paces from the road. But the "circle" is over an acre large and looks more like an abandoned field. Tall weeds choke the dirt road and scrape against the sides of the car. It doesn't help either that I step out into an active ant hill.

"I don't know about y'all," I say, "but I don't even believe this." I am used to the haphazard cemetery-keeping that is traditional in most southern Black communities, but this neglect is staggering. As far as I can see there is nothing but bushes and weeds, some as tall as my waist. One grave is near the road, and Charlotte elects to investigate it. It is fairly clean, and belongs to someone who died in 1963.

Rosalee and I plunge into the weeds; I pull my long dress up to my hips. The weeds scratch my knees, and the insects have a feast. Looking back, I see Charlotte standing resolutely near the road.

"Aren't you coming?" I call.

"No," she calls back. "I'm from these parts and I know what's out there." She means snakes.

"Shit," I say, my whole life and the people I love flashing melodramatically before my eyes. Rosalee is a few yards to my right.

"How're you going to find anything out here?" she asks. And I stand still a few seconds, looking at the weeds. Some of them are quite pretty, with tiny yellow flowers. They are thick and healthy, but dead weeds under them have formed a thick gray carpet on the ground. A snake could be lying six inches from my big toe and I wouldn't see it. We move slowly, very slowly, our eyes alert, our legs trembly. It is hard to tell where the center of the circle is since the circle is not really round, but more like half of something round. There are things crackling and hissing in the grass. Sandspurs are sticking to the inside of my skirt. Sand and ants cover my feet. I look toward the road and notice that there are, indeed, *two* large curving stones, making an entrance and exit to the cemetery. I take my bearings from them and try to navigate to exact center. But the center of anything can be very large, and a grave is not a pinpoint. Finding the grave seems positively hopeless. There is only one thing to do:

"Zora!" I yell, as loud as I can (causing Rosalee to jump). "Are you out here?"

"If she is, I sho hope she don't answer you. If she do, I'm gone."

"Zora!" I call again. "I'm here. Are you?"

"If she is," grumbles Rosalee, "I hope she'll keep it to herself."

"Zora!" Then I start fussing with her. "I hope you don't think I'm going to stand out here all day, with these snakes watching me and these ants having a field day. In fact, I'm going to call you just one or two more times." On a clump of dried grass, near a small bushy tree, my eye falls on one of the largest bugs I have ever seen. It is on its back, and is as large as three of my fingers. I walk toward it, and yell "Zo-ra!" and my foot sinks into a hole. I look down. I am standing in a sunken rectangle that is about six feet long and about three or four feet wide. I look up to see where the two gates are.

"Well," I say, "this is the center, or approximately anyhow. It's also the only sunken spot we've found. Doesn't this look like a grave to you?"

"For the sake of not going no farther through these bushes," Rosalee growls, "yes, it do."

"Wait a minute," I say, "I have to look around some more to be sure this is the only spot that resembles a grave. But you don't have to come."

Rosalee smiles—a grin, really—beautiful and tough.

"Naw," she says, "I feels sorry for you. If one of these snakes got ahold of you out here by yourself I'd feel *real* bad." She laughs. "I done come this far, I'll go on with you."

"Thank you, Rosalee," I say. "Zora thanks you, too."

"Just as long as she don't try to tell me in person," she says, and together we walk down the field.

The gusto and flavor of Zora Neal[e] Hurston's story-telling, for example, long before the yarns were published in "Mules and Men" and other books, became a local legend, which might . . . have spread further under different conditions. A tiny shift in the center of gravity could have made them best-sellers.

—*Arna Bontemps,* Personals

Bitter over the rejection of her folklore's value, especially in the Black community, frustrated by what she felt was her failure to convert the Afro-American world view into the forms of prose fiction, Hurston finally gave up.

—*Robert Hemenway*

When Charlotte and I drive up to the Merritt Monument Company, I immediately see the headstone I want.

"How much is this one?" I ask the young woman in charge, pointing to a tall black stone. It looks as majestic as Zora herself must have been when she was learning voodoo from those root doctors down in New Orleans.

"Oh, *that* one," she says, "that's our finest. That's Ebony Mist."

"Well, how much is it?"

"I don't know. But wait," she says, looking around in relief, "here comes somebody who'll know."

A small, sunburned man with squinty green eyes comes up. He must be the engraver, I think, because his eyes are contracted into slits, as if he has been keeping stone dust out of them for years.

"That's Ebony Mist," he says. "That's our best."

"How much is it?" I ask, beginning to realize I probably *can't* afford it.

He gives me a price that would feed a dozen Sahelian drought victims for three years. I realize I must honor the dead, but between the dead great and the living starving, there is no choice.

"I have a lot of letters to be engraved," I say, standing by the plain gray marker I have chosen. It is pale and ordinary, not at all like Zora, and makes me momentarily angry that I am not rich.

We go into his office and I hand him a sheet of paper that has:

Zora Neale Hurston
"A Genius of the South"
Novelist Folklorist
Anthropologist
1901   1960

"A genius of the South" is from one of Jean Toomer's poems.

"Where is this grave?" the monument man asks. "If it's in a new cemetery, the stone has to be flat."

"Well, it's not a new cemetery and Zora—my aunt—doesn't need anything flat, because with the weeds out there, you'd never be able to see it. You'll have to go out there with me."

He grunts.

"And take a long pole and 'sound' the spot," I add. "Because there's no way of telling it's a grave, except that it's sunken."

"Well," he says, after taking my money and writing up a receipt, in the full awareness that he's the only monument dealer for miles, "you take this flag" (he hands me a four-foot-long pole with a red-metal marker on top) "and take it out to the cemetery and put it where you think the grave is. It'll take us about three weeks to get the stone out there."

I wonder if he knows he is sending me to another confrontation with the snakes. He probably does. Charlotte has told me she will cut my leg and suck out the blood if I am bit.

"At least send me a photograph when it's done, won't you?"

He says he will.

Hurston's return to her folklore-collecting in December of 1927 was made possible by Mrs. R. Osgood Mason, an elderly White patron of the arts, who at various times also helped Langston Hughes, Alain Locke, Richmond Barthe, and Miguel Covarrubias. Hurston apparently came to her attention through the intercession of Locke, who frequently served as a kind of liaison between the young Black talent and Mrs. Mason. The entire relationship between this woman and the Harlem Renaissance deserves extended study, for it represents much of the ambiguity involved in White patronage of Black artists. All her artists were instructed to call her "Godmother"; there was a decided emphasis on the "primitive" aspects of Black culture, apparently a holdover from Mrs. Mason's interest in the Plains Indians. In Hurston's case there were special restrictions imposed by her patron: although she was to be paid a handsome salary for her folklore collecting, she was to limit her correspondence and publish nothing of her research without prior approval.

—*Robert Hemenway*

You have to read the chapters Zora *left out* of her autobiography.

—*Student, Special Collections Room,*
Beinecke Library, Yale University

Dr. Benton, a friend of Zora's and a practicing M.D. in Fort Pierce, is one of those old, good-looking men whom I always have trouble not liking. (It no longer bothers me that I may be constantly searching for father figures; by this time, I have found several and dearly enjoyed knowing them all.) He is shrewd, with steady brown eyes under hair that is almost white. He is probably in his seventies, but doesn't look it. He carries himself with dignity, and has cause to be proud of the new clinic where he now practices medicine. His nurse looks at us with suspicion, but Dr. Benton's eyes have the penetration of a scalpel cutting through skin. I guess right away that if he knows anything at all about Zora Hurston, he will not believe I am her niece. "Eatonville?" Dr. Benton says, leaning forward in his chair, looking first at me, then at Charlotte. "Yes, I know Eatonville; I grew up not far from there. I knew the whole bunch of Zora's family." (He looks at the shape of my cheekbones, the size of my eyes, and the nappiness of my hair.) "I knew her daddy. The old man. He was a hard-working, Christian man. Did the best he could for his family. He was the mayor of Eatonville for a while, you know.

"My father was the mayor of Goldsboro. You probably never heard of it. It never incorporated like Eatonville did, and has just about disappeared. But Eatonville is still all Black."

He pauses and looks at me. "And you're Zora's niece," he says wonderingly.

"Well," I say with shy dignity, yet with some tinge, I hope, of a nineteenth-century blush, "I'm illegitimate. That's why I never knew Aunt Zora."

I love him for the way he comes to my rescue. "You're *not* illegitimate!" he cries, his eyes resting on me fondly. "All of us are God's children! Don't you even *think* such a thing!"

And I hate myself for lying to him. Still, I ask myself, would I have gotten this far toward getting the headstone and finding out about Zora Hurston's last days without telling my lie? Actually, I probably would have. But I don't like taking chances that could get me stranded in central Florida.

"Zora didn't get along with her family. I don't know why. Did you read her autobiography, *Dust Tracks on a Road*?"

"Yes, I did," I say. "It pained me to see Zora pretending to be naive and grateful about the old White 'Godmother' who helped finance her research, but I loved the part where she ran off from home after falling out with her brother's wife."

Dr. Benton nods. "When she got sick, I tried to get her to go back to her family, but she refused. There wasn't any real hatred; they just never had gotten along and Zora wouldn't go to them. She didn't want to go to the county home, either, but she had to, because she couldn't do a thing for herself."

"I was surprised to learn she died of malnutrition."

Dr. Benton seems startled. "Zora *didn't* die of malnutrition," he says indignantly. "Where did you get that story from? She had a stroke and she died in the welfare home." He seems peculiarly upset, distressed, but sits back reflectively in his chair. "She was an incredible woman," he muses. "Sometimes when I closed my office, I'd go by her house and just talk to her for an hour or two. She was a well-read, well-traveled woman and always had her own ideas about what was going on. . . ."

"I never knew her, you know. Only some of Carl Van Vechten's photographs and some newspaper photographs . . . What did she look like?"

"When I knew her, in the fifties, she was a big woman, *erect*. Not quite as light as I am [Dr. Benton is dark beige], and about five foot, seven inches, and she weighed about two hundred pounds. Probably more. She . . ."

"What! Zora was *fat*! She wasn't, in Van Vechten's pictures!"

"Zora loved to eat," Dr. Benton says complacently. "She could sit down with a mound of ice cream and just eat and talk till it was all gone."

While Dr. Benton is talking, I recall that the Van Vechten pictures were taken when Zora was still a young woman. In them she appears tall, tan, and healthy. In later newspaper photographs—when she was in her forties—I remembered that she seemed heavier and several shades lighter. I reasoned that the earlier photographs were taken while she was busy collecting folklore materials in the hot Florida sun.

"She had high blood pressure. Her health wasn't good. . . . She used to live in one of my houses—on School Court Street. It's a block house. . . . I don't recall the number. But my wife and I used to invite her over to the house for dinner. *She always ate well*," he says emphatically.

"That's comforting to know," I say, wondering where Zora ate when she wasn't with the Bentons.

"Sometimes she would run out of groceries—after she got sick—and she'd call me. 'Come over here and see 'bout me,' she'd say. And I'd take her shopping and buy her groceries.

"She was always studying. Her mind—before the stroke—just worked all the time. She was always going somewhere, too. She once went to Honduras to study something. And when she died, she was working on that book about Herod the Great. She was so intelligent! And really had perfect expressions. Her English was beautiful." (I suspect this is a clever way to let me know Zora herself didn't speak in the "Black English" her characters used.)

"I used to read all of her books," Dr. Benton continues, "but it was a long time ago. I remember one about . . . it was called, I think, *The Children of God* [*Their Eyes Were Watching God*], and I remember Janie and Teapot [Teacake] and the mad dog riding on the cow in that hurricane and bit old Teapot on the cheek. . . ."

I am delighted that he remembers even this much of the story, even if the names are wrong, but seeing his affection for Zora I feel I must ask him about her burial. "Did she *really* have a pauper's funeral?"

"She *didn't* have a pauper's funeral!" he says with great heat. "Everybody around here *loved* Zora."

"We just came back from ordering a headstone," I say quietly, because he *is* an old man and the color is coming and going on his face, "but to tell the truth, I can't be positive what I found is the grave. All I know is the spot I found was the only grave-size hole in the area."

"I remember it wasn't near the road," says Dr. Benton, more calmly. "Some other lady came by here and we went out looking for the grave and I took a long iron stick and poked all over that part of the cemetery but we didn't find anything. She took some pictures of the general area. Do the weeds still come up to your knees?"

"And beyond," I murmur. This time there isn't any doubt. Dr. Benton feels ashamed.

As he walks us to our car, he continues to talk about Zora. "She couldn't really write much near the end. She had the stroke and it left her weak; her mind was affected. She couldn't think about anything for long.

"She came here from Daytona, I think. She owned a house-boat over there. When she came here, she sold it. She lived on that money, then she worked as a maid—for an article on maids she was writing—and she worked for the *Chronicle* writing the horoscope column.

"I think Black people here in Florida got mad at her because she was for some politician they were against. She said this politician *built* schools for Blacks while the one they wanted just talked about it. And although Zora wasn't egotistical, what she thought, she thought; and generally what she thought, she said."

When we leave Dr. Benton's office, I realize I have missed my plane back home to Jackson, Mississippi. That being so, Charlotte and I decide to find the house Zora lived in before she was taken to the county welfare home to die. From among her many notes, Charlotte locates a letter of Zora's she has copied that carries the address: 1734 School Court Street. We ask several people for directions. Finally, two old gentlemen in a dusty gray Plymouth offer to lead us there. School Court Street is not paved, and the road is full of mud puddles. It is dismal and squalid, redeemed only by the brightness of the late afternoon sun. Now I can understand what a "block" house is.

It is a house shaped like a block, for one thing, surrounded by others just like it. Some houses are blue and some are green or yellow. Zora's is light green. They are tiny—about fifty by fifty feet, squatty with flat roofs. The house Zora lived in looks worse than the others, but that is its only distinction. It also has three ragged and dirty children sitting on the steps.

"Is this where y'all live?" I ask, aiming my camera.

"No, ma'am," they say in unison, looking at me earnestly. "We live over yonder. This Miss So-and-So's house; but she in the horspital."

We chatter inconsequentially while I take more pictures. A car drives up with a young Black couple in it. They scowl fiercely at Charlotte and don't look at me with friendliness, either. They get out and stand in their doorway across the street. I go up to them to explain. "Did you know Zora Hurston used to live right across from you?" I ask.

"Who?" They stare at me blankly, then become curiously attentive, as if they think I made the name up. They are both Afroed and he is somberly dashikied.

I suddenly feel frail and exhausted. "It's too long a story," I say, "but tell me something: is there anybody on this street who's lived here for more than thirteen years?"

"That old man down there," the young man says, pointing. Sure enough, there is a man sitting on his steps three houses down. He has graying hair and is very neat, but there is a weakness about him. He reminds me of Mrs. Turner's husband in *Their Eyes Were Watching God.* He's rather "vanishing"-looking, as if his features have been sanded down. In the old days, before Black was beautiful, he was probably considered attractive, because he has wavy hair and light brown skin; but now, well, light skin has ceased to be its own reward.

After the preliminaries, there is only one thing I want to know: "Tell me something," I begin, looking down at Zora's house. "Did Zora like flowers?"

He looks at me queerly. "As a matter of fact," he says, looking regretfully at the bare, rough yard that surrounds her former house, "she was crazy about them. And she was a great gardener. She loved azaleas, and that running and blooming vine [morning-glories], and she really loved that night-smelling flower [gardenia]. She kept a vegetable garden year-round, too. She raised collards and tomatoes and things like that.

"Everyone in this community thought well of Miss Hurston. When she died, people all up and down this street took up a collection for her burial. We put her away nice."

"Why didn't somebody put up a headstone?"

"Well, you know, one was never requested. Her and her family didn't get along. They didn't even come to the funeral."

"And did she live down there by herself?"

"Yes, until they took her away. She lived with—just her and her companion, Sport."

My ears perk up. "Who?"

"Sport, you know, her dog. He was her only companion. He was a big brown-and-white dog."

When I walk back to the car, Charlotte is talking to the young couple on their porch. They are relaxed and smiling.

"I told them about the famous lady who used to live across the street from them," says Charlotte as we drive off. "Of course they had no idea Zora ever lived, let alone that she lived across the street. I think I'll send some of her books to them."

"That's real kind of you," I say.

I am not tragically colored. There is no great sorrow dammed up in my soul, nor lurking behind my eyes. I do not mind at all. I do not belong to the sobbing school of Negrohood who hold that nature somehow has given them a lowdown dirty deal and whose feelings are all hurt about it. . . . No, I do not weep at the world—I am too busy sharpening my oyster knife.

> —*Zora Neale Hurston,*
> *"How It Feels to Be Colored*
> *Me,"* World Tomorrow, *1928*

There are times—and finding Zora Hurston's grave was one of them—when normal responses of grief, horror, and so on do not make sense because they bear no real relation to the depth of the emotion one feels. It was impossible for me to cry when I saw the field full of weeds where Zora is. Partly this is because I have come to know Zora through her books and she was not a teary sort of person herself; but partly, too, it is because there is a point at which even grief feels absurd. And at this point, laughter gushes up to retrieve sanity.

It is only later, when the pain is not so direct a threat to one's own existence, that what was learned in that moment of comical lunacy is understood. Such moments rob us of both youth and vanity. But perhaps they are also times when greater disciplines are born.

1975

THE BRASS BED

pearl cleage

The lineage runs through the women. Because of the children. And the bed. Or maybe that's saying the same thing twice. Or once removed. No matter. It was a lot of different things for the men. Mostly land. Sometimes drinking. Every once in a while, gambling. But for the women, it was always because of the children that they made a move or didn't. Left a man or stayed. Their choices were more limited.

The problem is in getting ahead of the story, or refusing to get behind it, or thinking there is no story. Begin at the beginning.

It was 1885, give or take a year on either side. There were thirteen sisters and their mother had been born a slave. Abbie and Jennie were the oldest and the youngest, respectively, and they lived outside of Montgomery, Alabama.

Their mother was a seamstress and they spent their days bent over bolts of New York silk, translating the latest in Paris styles into an acceptable Alabama facsimile for the genteel

White ladies who oohed and aahed over the fineness of their stitches and bemoaned the rising cost of southern chic.

It was hard work and their mother demanded silence to insure concentration. After a few years of this, Abbie, in a fit of passion and defiance, married herself off to a riverboat gambler with a dimple in his chin and a cruel mouth who beat her, threw her children into the street, and locked the door behind them. He traveled the Mississippi bringing home not money for food and children's clothing, but trunks of satin dresses, thick golden rings, diamond studs, and bottles of expensive cognac.

In a poker game on one such trip, he badly beat a hard-eyed man without a sense of humor, who waited until he slept and then slit his throat from ear to ear. Frightened and alone, Abbie became the mistress of the town sheriff, who bought her a small house on the outskirts of town so that he could visit her in safety, away from the eyes of his White family. She felt safe there, until the sheriff was killed by a man who made his living selling moonshine whiskey.

Desperate and weary, Abbie went to live with her sister, who, by this time, had married a musician, presented him with two daughters, and watched him die of stab wounds at a church barbecue that got out of hand. It was too much. Abbie and Jennie, clutching their few belongings and their children, fled Alabama in the midst of a summer yellow fever quarantine and settled, breathless and amazed, in Detroit, Michigan.

Jennie soon returned to Alabama, frightened more of the North and its grime than the South and its fevers. She married one last time to a small, very jealous Italian who hid himself on the street, watching her pass undetected, making sure she walked alone. He fathered her last child, Alice, who contracted polio as an infant and carried a small, twisted leg as a reminder for the rest of her life.

Jennie's oldest daughter, Fannie, was a bright girl who helped out in the grocery store owned by an uncle once removed. She was well-known in the neighborhood for her ability to add long columns of numbers in her head, rapidly and without error. She remembered many years later the off-color remarks of the White men who came to the store to tease and transact business with the slender, green-eyed Black girl. "I would just press my lips together," she remembered, "and look north."

Looking north with the same hopeful eyes was a certain Mershell C. Graham, a hardworking, sober, Christian man who was looking for a good woman to share his life and bear his children. Fannie promised to wait for him, and he went north, to Detroit, at Abbie's urging, found the job at Ford's that he would keep for the next forty years, and saved his money so he could send for his fiancée.

One day in the midst of his waiting, he passed by two policemen setting furniture out on the street from a recently raided whorehouse. They set a bed down in front of Mershell, swore softly at each other, and went back inside. He had not been in the market for a bed, but this one, *this* one, was made of thick highly polished brass and when Mershell saw it, magnificently blocking his path home, he reached into his pocket, peeled off five one-dollar bills, and rescued the bed from an unknown fate. He soon sent for Fannie and went about settling down to raise a family, being careful, of course, never to tell his wife that the fine brass bed in which all four of her children were conceived had first been home to the more practiced moves of big-city whores and their johns.

Shell and Fannie had four children: two sons and two daughters. One son died at the age of three of scarlet fever, and the other was run over by a truck a few blocks from home and died in the street, calling for his mother.

Mershell and his youngest daughter were once hit by a train, which he could not see because of one blind eye, the result of a hunting accident. His daughter, who saw the train coming, was too embarrassed to mention it to him for fear his feelings might be hurt because he could not see it for himself and remove her from danger. No matter. They were not hurt and walked home, exhilarated by the adventure and assuring Fannie that yes, they were still very much alive. Yes, yes. They were very much alive.

Jennie missed her sister and her daughter and soon moved to Detroit with her two remaining daughters, Daisy Pearl and Alice. They found work as seamstresses in a fine fur store downtown sewing purple silk linings in midnight sable coats.

In poor health now, Jennie kept their house for them and spent the last years of her life fussing and giving orders from a wheelchair. When Jennie died, she left a space in the lives of their spinster daughters that they filled with her memory and regular Wednesday night cards with a few female friends.

One evening, Alice and Daisy had dinner, played a gentle game of dominos, drank a small glass of sweet red wine between them, and retired to the double bed they had shared since they were children. In the morning, Alice found Daisy sleeping rather more heavily than usual, but did not wake her. Two days later, she called Fannie, asking in a whisper for her advice on the matter. When the funeral home came for the body, the small house was sickly sweet with Alice's efforts to divert the truth with a dark blue bottle of *Evening in Paris* cologne.

Alice moved in with Fannie after that, but she was never the same. She had come to occupy that position she dreaded most, the spinster sister come to live alone in an upstairs room, memories taped to the edges of her mirror. But she spared herself that loneliness. She fled from that upstairs room by refusing to believe that she was there at all. Family dinners became tense with Alice giggling at someone no one else could see. Alice, muffling laughter in her hand, whispering: "Please don't make me laugh! You know they can't hear you!"

After a while, they put her in an institution and visited her every other Sunday, until Fannie died, and then it didn't seem to matter much anymore. Alice didn't live long after that. Her death passed through the family with barely noticeable murmurs.

Jennie Turner is my great-grandmother, Abbie Allen my great-great-aunt, Mershell and Fannie Graham my maternal grandparents. All gone now. Except what they remembered and told. And except the brass bed from the house of ill repute. It now belongs to me.

TO MISS IDA BEE
WITH LOVE

miriam decosta-willis

I never dreamed when I picked up a copy of Dorothy Sterling's *Black Foremothers* in 1979 that my life would become so entangled with that of Ida B. Wells. In the past seventeen years I have read and written about this remarkable woman, given papers and lectures on her life and work, and edited *The Memphis Diary of Ida B. Wells,* which she wrote between 1885 and 1887. Although more than a hundred years separate us, I have come to know her well. She was a complex and intensely private woman, who distanced herself emotionally—even from those she loved the most.

So many times in the past six years, I have asked myself: What would Ida B. Wells think about my editing and publishing a diary in which she exposes all of her vulnerabilities—her fears, insecurities, weaknesses, and frustrations? I think that she would have had two reactions. Because she was a somewhat vain and rather self-centered woman, as are many charismatic leaders, she would have been delighted to see herself in print. On the other hand, she would have insisted on censoring some of my editorial comments, particularly my speculations about her sexual inexperience, predilection for men, and seeming disdain for women.

I have also asked myself frequently: If I had lived during her lifetime, would I have liked Ida B. Wells and would we have been friends? Although I began my research in awe of her, for Wells is an icon of African American history and a formidable woman who single-handedly organized an international campaign against lynching, I discovered a private person with whom I shared many similarities. We had the same ambition and drive, tenacity and stubbornness, temper and sharp tongue, even the same aloofness and self-absorption. How could I not have liked Wells? I understood her. We were cut from the same cloth—each male-identified and the eldest daughter and favorite child of a strong, dominant father. Also, our worldviews were shaped by the Protestant work ethic and New England (missionary) Puritanism, Wells at Rust University and me at a northern preparatory school and college.

Our lives converge in interesting ways. Both us have been teachers, writers, feminists, militants, wives, and mothers, but we have different life histories. Wells, a long-distance runner, remained in the struggle for racial and gender equality, while after a decade of exhausting activism, I chose a contemplative life of writing about race and gender. Wells taught in Memphis during the post-Reconstruction period, when public schools were segregated and teaching was difficult; I became a college teacher in Memphis during the civil rights movement when opportunities for Black women were opening up. We made different choices in our personal lives. She was more adventurous and less conventional in her early years, while I became a risk taker at midlife. As a young woman, she wrote, traveled abroad, attended conferences, edited and bought two newspapers, met exciting and accomplished men, and delayed marriage and childbearing. Not until her thirties did she settle down, marrying a prominent lawyer and raising four children. At twenty I married a lawyer, had four children by thirty, divorced, married another lawyer, and, after his death, became an adventurous older woman.

Given all the parallels, Wells and I certainly would have been friends . . . but not *close* friends, because she had a reserve and formality that I would have found daunting. She was a serious woman whose entire life was devoted to the "cause." Although she went to parties, picnics, and even baseball games in her twenties, she had little time for frivolous pursuits after launching a career and marrying. In an interview with Dorothy Sterling, Wells's daughter, Alfreda Duster, shared: "Mother used the telephone for business, but didn't talk long. She didn't have any social friends, folks who just came by to talk." As far as I can tell, Wells had no close women friends, so I can't imagine calling her on the telephone to chitchat or inviting her to lift weights with me at the health club. If Ida B. Wells had lived during my lifetime, I would have tried to break through that reserve and formality to connect with the spunky, partygoing woman whom I came to know, to like, and even to love in the pages of her diary.

A friend once asked me if my feelings about Wells changed as I edited the diary, and they did. Initially I felt tremendous respect and admiration (which I still do), but an interesting thing happens when you explore the text(s) of a person's life. You are drawn into a close, almost spiritual relationship with that person. This first happened to me in college, when I spent months reading the works of a nineteenth-century novelist for my senior thesis. During a period of intense writing, I began to dream in Spanish, and one night I dreamed that the statue of Benito Pérez Galdós turned and spoke to me. That dream, still vivid after so many years, suggested to me that we were kindred souls, united in a labor of love. And so it was with Ida B. Wells. As I turned the pages of her letters, autobiography, essays, newspaper articles, and three diaries, searching for the woman behind the text, I could almost feel her peering over my shoulder, nodding approvingly when I revealed that Stella B. was her cousin and frowning disapprovingly when I disclosed that she was rumored to be the mistress of Reverend Nightingale.

When I began this essay about my relationship with Ida B. Wells, I felt intuitively that it should take the form of letters, because I am and she was an incessant letter writer. The epistolary form also seemed appropriate because letters and diaries— both of which are open, intimate, and informal texts—have been traditionally two of the most important genres in women's literature. In these letters to Ida Bee (as I call her affectionately), I explore the evolution of our friendship and reconstruct my long engagement with the text(s) of her life.

October 17, 1989

Dear Miss Wells:

Your words haunted me the other night as I headed up Route 66 from Fairfax, Virginia, making my twice weekly journey back to Washington after a long day of teaching. You wrote, "I thought I had exorcised the demon." (Uhhh-hunh, I mused knowingly, as I pressed down on the accelerator.) It was a dark and moonless night, illuminated only by the glare of headlights speeding in the opposite direction. Suspended in that dark void outside of time and space, I realized that I was pursued by the same demon.

I remembered the morning. I had just stepped out of the tub and was dressing for work, when the package arrived—a flat cardboard box containing a photocopy of your diary. Excited and more than a little curious, I sat down to skim the diary while finishing my second cup of coffee. It was 9:23 and I had to leave by 11:00, so I decided to read a few pages. Your first words, written on December 29, 1885, intrigued me: "I am this day seated in a room of the Rust University. . . . How strange everything seems!" I can see you there—not in a bedroom or kitchen, like most women of the period, but in a classroom!—and I can feel your estrangement. (Do you think it's true that you can't go back home again?) You were different from that girl who dropped out of Rust in 1878. Seven years older, you had left behind old friends and painful memories to make a new life for yourself in Memphis.

As I read on, I got caught up in the details of your life: the constant moves from one boardinghouse to another, the buying sprees in Mencken's Palatial Emporium, and the trials and tribulations of teaching at the Saffarans School. On page 83, I discovered that you returned to Holly Springs in June 1886. Well, I told myself, I'll just read a few more pages and find out what happened on your next visit. In the entry of June 12, you wrote, insightfully, about how tempestuous, rebellious, and hardheaded you were, but I like you so much more than your classmate Annie, who seems bland and insipid with her "obedient disposition, extreme tractableness, and ladylike refinement." I bet the demure Annie didn't own a pistol, organize an antilynching campaign, or march in a suffrage parade.

By now it was 10:15 and I barely had time to dress and dash off to school, but I had to find out about your trip west that summer. I discovered that you ended up in California but couldn't decide whether to stay there, move to Missouri, or return to Tennessee. Finally, you resigned your job and sent a telegram to Kansas City: "Leaving tonight. If too late to secure position there, will go on to Memphis." I thought to myself: When Ida B. Wells decided to move, she didn't mess around.

At 11:20, I flew out of the door, certain that I'd be late for my 1:00 o'clock intermediate Spanish class. While the students conjugated irregular subjunctives, I kept replaying your words in my head about exorcising the demon of unrest and dissatisfaction.

> Sincerely yours,
> Miriam DeCosta-Willis

In this first letter, I tried to recapture the feelings of anticipation and tremendous excitement that I experienced when I received the copy of Wells's diary.

October 27, 1989

Dear Miss Wells:

This is just a short note to let you know that I finished reading the diary the night after receiving it, because I couldn't wait to find out what happened on your return to Memphis that summer.

It was so interesting to read details about some of the people and places that I have studied and written about in the past twenty years: places like the Congregational Church (which I joined) and LeMoyne Normal Institute (now LeMoyne-Owen College, where I taught); men and women like Mary Church, a graduate of Oberlin College; Green Polonius Hamilton, who wrote two books about Black Memphians; Taylor Nightingale, a minister and editor of the *Free Speech and Headlight*; and Josiah T. Settle, your landlord, who was one of the first Black attorneys in the city.

You recount some fascinating details about those people. I couldn't believe that J. T. Settle had the nerve to reprimand you for "playing with edged tools" in your relationships with men. Who did he think he was? Your father? (It was ironic that a few days later you let Louis Brown kiss you twice—verboten for a Victorian maiden!) And Theresa Settle, whom you describe as so genteel and ladylike, had the audacity to lock up your things because she claimed that you owed her $18. (You know, of course, that after Theresa's death, her husband married Fannie McCollough, the music teacher at LeMoyne? No? Well, maybe that happened after you left Memphis in 1892.) By the way, I was happy to find out that you returned the $100 that you borrowed from Robert R. Church Sr., because his family, including his granddaughter Roberta Church (who died unexpectedly last summer in Memphis), were well-respected, quite proper people of color. Even so, I was surprised that he lent you so much money without even knowing you.

What shocked me, though, was to learn that your longtime beau, I. J. Graham, got married on you after all those months of visits, parties, and Parcheesi games . . . and you were so cool about it. "Mr. G. was married very unexpectedly last week," was how you put it, before adding, "I wish him joy." If I hadn't figured out that G., Mr. G., I. J. G., and Mr. Graham all referred to the public school teacher with whom you were rumored to be having an "immoral" relationship (Memphians can be so catty and provincial sometimes!), I would have missed the impact of your announcement.

This note has become a little lengthy, so more later.

Sincerely,
Miriam D.-W.

In the following letter, I was able to reconstruct the dates and stages in my research on Wells by turning to my journal, where I recorded my work-in-progress.

January 10, 1990

Dear Miss I. B. Wells:

Well, I'm back in Memphis, where I've decided to spend my semester break working on a paper, based on your diary, to present at a meeting of the Southern Conference of African American Studies here in February.

I spent most of the holidays in the Memphis/Shelby County Library on the corner of Peabody and McLean, where I consulted journal articles, master's theses, dissertations, and standard books on local history. I enjoyed chatting with Jim Johnson, head of the library's history department, who gave me access to microfilms of nineteenth-century newspapers, city directories, and census reports. Many of the books that were most useful, however, including G. P. Hamilton's *The Bright Side of Memphis*, Roberta Church and Ronald Walter's *Nineteenth Century Memphis Families of Color, 1850–1900*, and David M. Tucker's *Black Pastors and Leaders*, were in my own library.

I can't tell you the thrill I received when I found an interesting tidbit that illuminated some item in your diary. For example, I located a description of the Kortretch School (formerly the Clay Street School, where you taught) in the July 13, 1886, issue of the *Daily Appeal*, and I found you listed—dressed to the nines, of course: "Miss Ida B. Wells, blue surrah lace overdress"—in an account of the Live Oak Club's 1889 banquet, reproduced in *Families of Color*.

I just know that this is going to be a great year!

Sincerely,
Miriam

Increasingly, I became intrigued by the way Wells represented herself in her various texts and by others' representations (or, in her view, their "misrepresentations") of her. As I
examined these contradictory images, I realized that Wells was
a complex woman, an innocent "butterfly" on the one hand
and a rebellious crusader on the other.

February 28, 1990

Dear Miss Wells:

I'm back in Washington after an exciting few days in Memphis, where I presented a paper, "Ida B. Wells's Diary: A Narrative of the Black Community of Memphis in the 1880s." The
audience, composed of conference participants as well as
LeMoyne-Owen faculty and students, loved the paper, especially when I set aside the dry, scholarly script and took on the
Wells persona with "hands on hip, letting my backbone slip."
The ladies really identified with Miss Ida Bee, the clothes-
horse, who spent half a month's salary on one lovely, lined silk
dress. I waxed dramatic when I got to the line "My expenses are
transcending my income: I must stop." Of course we knew that
you didn't stop! The faculty smiled and the students grinned,
as if to say "Black folk sure love to style." People practically
clapped when I quoted you: "I did not resist the impulse to buy
that cloak: I would have been $15 richer."

Anyone who looks at your photographs must be aware that
you loved to dress and then to pose—all decked out in ribbons
and bows—for those "cabinets" that you sent all over the
country. My favorite (which I'll use on the cover of the diary) is
the "Portrait of Iola" that appeared in I. Garland Penn's the
Afro-American Press. Your hair is beautifully coiffed in a pom-
padour and side sweep, topped by a crown of gold beads. You

are wearing a beaded velvet neckband that underscores your low décolletage (go, girl!), and your elegant black velvet dress is decorated with white geometric figures from which beaded threads cascade. You have the regal look of the woman whom journalists dubbed the "Princess of the Press."

You know, I have several mental images of you, but my favorite is of the fearless fighter whom I called "Pistol-Packing Iola" in a paper I gave in 1984. (I presented the paper "Native Daughters as Writers and Witnesses: Ida B. Wells and Anne Moody" at a research conference at the University of Mississippi.) I had read that you bought a pistol after the mob destroyed your Memphis newspaper office and, later, insisted that "a Winchester rifle should have a place of honor in the home of every colored person." Honey, you were tough! Alfreda acknowledged your fearlessness when she wrote, "My mother always kept a gun in the house. When the 31st Street gang chased my brothers home one night, she dared anybody to cross her doorstep." A few mothers like you could clean up the streets of D.C.! Another image I have is of "Queen Bee," the lady who lay in bed until 10:00, had her tea and toast (oh, so British), read and wrote all day, and then waited for her husband to prepare dinner. A feminist after my own heart. You were used to being treated like royalty because you were crowned by Black journalists such as T. Thomas Fortune, I. Garland Penn, and William J. Simmons. (What is it about all those initials—T. and I. and J.? Is it a male thing or a nineteenth-century custom? Not to be outdone, you too insisted on your B., as in Ida B. Wells.)

I wonder which of these images of self you prefer.

All the best,
Miriam

My letters to Wells reflect the subtle changes in my feelings toward her as I began to see and understand the private woman behind the public figure. Expressions such as "honey" and "my dear," as well as changes in the salutations and closes of my letters, suggest that I began to like her as a person and to feel emotionally close to her.

July 10, 1990

Dear Miss I. B. W.,

I ran down to Holly Springs earlier this month to show a friend your birthplace. A professor of Black studies who uses your autobiography in one of his classes, Stanley was amazed that a godforsaken little Mississippi town could have produced a freedom fighter like you.

Well, my dear, the heat almost killed us! It must have been 105 degrees in the shade, so we hung out with the good ole boys in the café across from the courthouse because nothing, not even the dust, was moving in the streets. We were in the middle of southern "dog days." After a couple of barbecued ribs on light bread, we strolled—very, very slowly—around the town square, where posters announcing the Marshall County Kudzu Festival were evident in the stores and shops along the street. "What the hell" (excuse his French) "is kudzu?" Stanley asked. I laughed. "It's those big green vines that cover bushes and trees along the road. This part of the South is called Kudzu Country."

Other than a few landmarks that are mentioned in your diary, there are no monuments in Holly Springs to mark the life of its most illustrious daughter. We drove through the White section of town with its colonial houses, Greek revival mansions, and quaint churches—some of which were built before your birth in 1862. One of the streets leading west, away from the square, was lined with the barbershops, sundry stores, and juke joints that mark the fringes of the Black community. We took that street out to Rust College and then turned northwest toward Memphis. On the way back, Stanley asked, "Have you thought about publishing Wells's diary?" I had thought about it but needed some encouragement.

Maybe I'll get around to it one of these days.

Fondly,
Miriam

P.S. I just found out in looking through my Wells "Memorabilia" file that in May of this year a historical marker commemorating the 1892 lynching of the three Black grocers was dedicated in Memphis, and guess who unveiled the marker? None other than the first Black mayor of Holly Springs. Mississippi has definitely joined the Union.

In the following letter, I take Wells into my confidence as I would a close friend, confiding in her a weakness that I had not revealed to anyone—not even to myself.

July 20, 1990

Dear Miss Wells,

This is an addendum to my letter of July 10. In case you missed the implications of the final paragraph, I made a major confession there—that a *man* was the first person to encourage me to edit the diary for publication. Not only that, but I also asked Stanley to write the introduction. Actually, several men were very supportive of the project (but I didn't acknowledge all of them in my preface): historian Sterling Stuckey put me in touch with Professor Troy Duster, your grandson; attorney Benjamin Duster, writing on behalf of your family, granted me permission to publish the diary; and William Greaves, who produced a film on your life, sent an encouraging letter and a videotape of his documentary.

I write all this to say what? Well, in the process of editing your diary, I discovered something about myself that I suspected but never articulated: that I, too, am a very male-defined woman who needs the validation of men. In fact, it was that very trait that enabled me to understand the significance of your father—an activist and leader in politics and civil rights—in your development as a defiant and forceful race woman. When you wrote, "My earliest recollections are of reading the newspaper to my father," I thought of my strong attachment to my father, who also encouraged my academic and intellectual development. Ironically, your father, male mentors, and several Memphis men unwittingly helped you to construct a new paradigm of Black womanhood.

One of my friends, a feminist scholar, asked me point-blank: "What is your reaction to her practice of privileging males?" First of all, I have to say that your predilection for men is understandable given the lack of female role models in your early life, but what I don't understand is your apparent antipathy (perhaps that's too strong a word) toward women, particularly as you matured. You had a strong and loving mother, younger sisters, and two daughters, one of whom carried your name, but you wrote primarily about men: your father, brothers, and sons. You were aware of your difficulty in making and keeping women friends, for you wrote, "I have not kept the friends I have won." After you left Memphis, you met dynamic race women, such as Anna Julia Cooper and Josephine St. Pierre Ruffin; organized women's clubs, including the Alpha

Suffrage Club; and led a suffrage parade in Chicago. The only woman whom you openly admired in your diary, however, was Mary Church. You explained that you were drawn to her because she had the "same desires, hopes & ambitions," but the two of you never became close friends.

You seem ambivalent about friendships with women. On the one hand, you lament your lack of friends, but on the other hand, you write with such antipathy for women. You completely dismissed Annie, your bright, pretty ladylike classmate; and you described Lutie Rice, the California friend with whom you'd corresponded, as old, settled, hard, affected, isolated, and "lower than [you] had imagined." I have to confess that those portraits of women were unsettling to me. In spite of your views on friendship, I remain

> Your friend,
> Miriam

The chronological gap between this and the preceding letter illustrates changes in my priorities during the editing of Wells's diary.

> August 13, 1991

Dear I. B. W.,

I haven't written in over a year, primarily because I've been trying to complete another book, which I mailed off to the publisher a month ago. Although I haven't made much progress on the diary, several things have happened. Last spring, I prepared a book proposal, which I sent off to a publisher, and this summer, the editor received a very fine assessment of the project from an outside reader. Then, in early August, I made another trip to Holly Springs, where I spent the day at the library, searching through cemetery records, and at the Marshall County Historical Society, which has a tiny exhibit of Wells artifacts on the top floor. I found three or four photographs there that the curator will have copied for me.

Although my visit to Rust College was fairly unproductive because so many of the records were destroyed by fires, I found a very illuminating history of the institution, which revealed the impact of Rust in shaping your religious beliefs, ethical values, and moral principles. The words "the Methodist dream of a *Christian civilizing mission* to the Freedmen" resonate with me, because I grew up on the campuses of and taught for most of my life at historically Black colleges in the South, so I am aware of the strong, conservative, religious, life-as-service ideology of those White missionaries that must have influenced the Black uplift movement after the Civil War. Some of those colleges—even through the 1960s—had dress codes, mandatory chapel and church attendance, 9:00 o'clock curfews for female students, and strict rules regulating behavior between the sexes. No wonder you were so straitlaced in your romantic attachments!

Speaking about your love life, I was amazed at your ability to juggle three or four relationships at the same time; you became irate, however, when the men about town accused you of being a flirt and a shameless coquette. They did so with reason because you defied *all* of the rules: you flirted with men, dated every other night, didn't have a steady beau, rejected marriage, traveled without a chaperone, and went out with strangers in distant cities. What I admire about you, though, is your willingness to pay the price for your indiscretions and unconventional behavior; all of those rumors about your "immoral conduct" used to get you from time to time, but you kept on stepping! (Mary Helen Washington and I used to debate whether or not you were a virgin when you married at age thirty-three. She thought that you weren't because you were such a feisty, adventurous, and passionate young woman; I argued that you were because you had too much to lose—your career and reputation—in that conservative and repressive time in which you lived.) Nowadays the rules are more relaxed, but, honey, the double standard is alive and well in the 1990s!

Take care. All for now.

Fondly,
Miriam

When the diary was in press, my editor asked me to complete a questionnaire with questions such as "How relevant are the struggles of Ida B. Wells to twentieth-century women?" and "Being from the same city and struggling with similar problems in very different times, how different have your reactions and choices been from Wells's?" Those questions forced me to look at the diary through different eyes: those of the wife, mother, and teacher (me) who matured during the civil rights movement and those of young women, like my daughters, who live in the nineties. That was a very enlightening exercise.

October 25, 1991

Dear Miss W.,

I have just about completed a paper, "Exorcising the Demon of Her Unrest: Self-Representation in Ida B. Wells's *Diary*," which I will present at the conference of the Association for the Study of Afro-American Life and History in Washington. Writing this paper gives me an opportunity to explore some of the topics—language, textual silences, discursive

strategies, concepts of self, patriarchal ideology, and representations of Black womanhood—that I will address in my introduction to your diary.

As I wrote in my first letter, I was struck by the metaphor
with which you described the dynamics of your life during that
period: the restlessness, dissatisfaction, desire for change, and
constant movement. You were a single woman who had spent
your adolescence caring for younger siblings after the death of
your parents, and now you longed for a challenging career,
exciting travel, and educational opportunities. When I read
your diary, I was going through a similar passage from one stage
of life to another, and I had the same restlessness, adventur-
ousness, and boundless energy. I was single again after thirty
years of marriage and child rearing, and I wanted to make a
new life for myself: travel, write, change jobs, and move to a
different city.

Your words and experiences are so relevant to Black women
like me who live and love and work in the 1990s. We have some
of the same problems that you faced: financial woes, mounting
debts, inadequate housing, feelings of loneliness and depression, and troubled relationships with women and men. Like
many single, professional women who rebelled against domesticity and conventional female roles, you were mired in a high-
status but low-paying job, which was boring and unrewarding.
You wanted a stimulating and challenging career, but you had
not yet found an outlet for your creativity and intelligence. You
confronted issues, such as racial and sexual discrimination,
lack of educational opportunities, and unequal access to
employment, that still confront Black women. When I was
growing up in the South in the 1950s, I was forced to attend
segregated schools and was jailed for sitting in the "White"
section of a restaurant. I wonder, though, if the nightmare will

ever end? One of my daughters—also a single, Black professional woman—plans to file a suit against her former employer,
alleging sexual harassment and discrimination based on race
and gender.

Your diary has given both of us comfort and courage.

All the best,
Miriam

I come from a family in which women wear their long
names with pride and dignity. Our personal and family histories are inscribed in our nomenclature. My mother is Beautine
Bernice Mabel Parson Hubert DeCosta Lee; I am Miriam
Dolores "Laurie" DeCosta Sugarmon Willis DeCosta-Willis.
I'm fascinated by names that are given, chosen, taken, and
dropped. In the following letter I comment and signify on the
names of Ida Bell (or Belle) "Iola" Wells Wells-Barnett.

June 22, 1992

Dear Ida,

(I hope you don't mind my calling you by your first name,
but I feel that I know you rather well after reading repeatedly
about your trysts with Louis and your letters to Charlie. But
more about names later.)

First, let me update you, because things are in full swing
now. In January, Mary Helen Washington agreed to write the
foreword to your diary, and she gave me a lot of material—articles, letters, interviews—that had been passed on to her by
Dorothy Sterling. She also put me in touch with Sarah
Ducksworth, who's collecting your newspaper articles for publication. (I know you'll be pleased to see those in print.) I don't
have a publisher nailed down now, but I have several leads, and

I've been working night and day on the transcriptions and doing additional research in the library since my return to Memphis. Dorothy has agreed to write the afterword, for which I suggested that she might pull together her interviews with Alfreda.

Now, back to names. I've always been impressed with your determination to keep your family name (I hate the term "maiden" name, which, like "chastity belt," evokes a feudal world in which female worth is predicated on sexual inexperience), because it was as Ida B. *Wells* that you gained fame as a journalist and crusader. You were definitely ahead of your time in the adoption of a hyphenated name. Alfreda explained:

> My mother was very strong willed. She was known as Ida B. Wells, so, when she married, she became Ida B. Wells-Barnett. She kept her own name in order to be remembered for what she had done. She was always introduced that way. [I was not as progressive as you were, because I adopted my hyphenated name late in life, after two marriages and several name changes.]

Two other things intrigue me about your name: the "Ida" and the "B." Apparently your first name was passed down in your family because both you and your aunt Fannie named your daughters "Ida," in the same way that men's names carry over from one generation to the next. Now about that "B." I like to call you "Ida Bee" because (1) like you, it's so jaunty, (2) it evokes the image of Queen Bee, as I've mentioned before, and (3) it suggests the double names of Southern women such as Sally Ann, Lou Ella, and Missy Mae (shades of Zora). Of course, I realize that your middle name is not "Bee," but do you know, I had a hard time finding out what the "B" stands for. I read somewhere that it was "Baker"; your daughter said it was "Bell" (which Paula Giddings confirmed); but I have a hunch that you were named "Belle" after your mother's sister. There's no way, however, to prove it, because you sailed through life with just the capital "B" and a period.

Although, Miss Bee, a rose by any other name . . . as they say.

Warmly,
Miriam

P.S. Where on earth did you get the pseudonym "Iola"? You referred to yourself by that name in a newspaper article dated September 12, 1885, and, again, in your diary entry of February 2, 1886. It's the name of Frances Harper's heroine, but she didn't publish *Iola Leroy* until 1892. Is it a 19th-century, neo-classical name?

I realized when the tone of my letters changed from serious to sassy that I was violating strict rules of propriety. After all, Ida B. Wells is an older woman. Our elders, our ancestors, and our foremothers are addressed with reverence. However, I'm a mature woman dealing with a woman-in-the-text who is twenty-five years old. So, I continued to take liberties.

September 12, 1992

Dear Ida,

Whoops! I just received Dorothy's afterword and read Alfreda's comments: "Nobody except my father ever called her 'Ida.' Black women had been trying for two hundred years to be called 'Mrs.,' so it was a breach of etiquette to call her by her first name." Well, I went back to the computer and changed every "Ida" in my editorial comments to "Wells." Sorry about that, but I'll continue to call you "Ida" in my letters, if that's okay. So, until next time.

Your friend,
Miriam

As the editing process came to an end, I began to speculate on all the pieces of the puzzle that were lost in fires, discarded records, and the passage of time. I wanted Ida B. Wells to turn toward me as Pérez Galdós did many years ago; I wanted her to speak to me or answer my letters, but she never did, not even in my daydreams or nightmares. She was much too pragmatic a woman to practice channeling, clairvoyance, or astral projection. What a pity!

June 27, 1993

Dear Miss Bee,

During a ten-day trip to England in late May and early June, I thought frequently about your two trips to Britain in the 1890s to gain international support for your antilynching campaign. It seems that I am following, however belatedly, in your footsteps, but my purpose for traveling abroad was not as lofty as yours. I went solely to see the sights and kick up my heels after an exhausting year of teaching, but I returned to Memphis intent on spending the *entire* summer completing work on your diary.

The text is finally taking shape: I've divided it into three parts, which have titles; added Mary Helen's foreword and Dorothy's afterword, as well as several of your newspaper articles, which Sarah sent me; decided to include the short diaries of 1893 and 1930; and completed the preface and bibliography. Now I'm looking up photographs and last-minute references in the library, double-checking for accuracy every single word in my transcription, and writing the introduction, which I hope to finish by mid-July. (I'm also doing my own word processing, which is very cumbersome on this antique Apple IIE. I have about ten files on each of fourteen disks. The publisher is going to kill me!) Editing a diary, particularly one over a hundred years old, is tedious and time-consuming work.

In quiet moments of reflection—late at night or early in the morning—I ponder unanswered questions about your narrative. Things like: What prevented you from graduating from Rust University? Did you leave or were you expelled? Who were the "old enemies" and what were the "painful memories" that you alluded to on your return to the campus? What happened between you and James B. Combs while you were students at Rust? How did you feel when he took you to meet his wife and babies? Why were you so taciturn about your breakup with I. J. Graham? In other words, I want to know about all the silences in your text: the acts that you do not describe, the feelings that you do not elaborate on, and the people who disappeared from the pages of your text.

I wish so much that you could answer my letters.

Fondly,
Miriam

Almost five years elapsed between the receipt of the manuscript diary in the fall of 1989 and the submission to a publisher of the final draft of *The Diary of Ida B. Wells* in the winter of 1994. There were long periods when I did not work on it at all, because I was teaching, presenting papers, writing articles, and publishing other books. The academic life is a precarious balancing act. I have tried in these letters to explain the delays and to suggest something of the process involved in editing a diary for publication.

November 13, 1993

Dear Ida Bee,

I have wonderful news to report: I just signed a contract with Beacon Press for the publication of your diary. My editor, Deb Chasman, has been very supportive of the project since I first wrote her about it in 1991. If I make revisions and submit the final draft by January, *The Memphis Diary of Ida B. Wells* will be in the bookstores by January of 1995.

It's sad in a way to come to the end of a long journey, this exciting discovery that you and I have taken together. In the process of reading, editing, and interpreting your narrative, I have recalled people and events from my life as well as gained insight into myself. When Della Scott, editor of *Abafazi: The Simmons College Review of Women of African Descent*, asked me in an interview if I would consider editing another diary, I told her that I didn't think so. But in going through the material from Dorothy, I found part of another diary, written in the delicate, flowery script of a woman. When I asked Dorothy about it, she said, "Oh, my, I had no idea that that was in there. It's the diary of Mary Church Terrell, which her daughter gave me to read."

Isn't it ironic that, among your papers, there was the narrative of a sister Memphian who befriended you in 1887 but who, according to your autobiography, betrayed you twelve years later? You wrote so enthusiastically about your first visit with Mary Church: "I was greatly benefitted by my visit and only wish I had known her long ago. I shall not let the acquaintance slack. Indeed I shall write & invite her to come out here to see me."

Both of you left Memphis and went on to become noted writers, eloquent speakers, and dynamic leaders in the struggle to obtain equal rights for women and Blacks. But what might have become a close friendship between kindred souls disintegrated, instead, into a power struggle between two ambitious, competitive women. When Mary Church Terrell removed your name from the National Association of Colored Women's convention program, you concluded that "she had obeyed the dictates of women whom she did not know against one she did know, who had come from her own home in Memphis, Tennessee."

One of the most important things that I have learned in editing your diary is the importance of friendships—with women and men. It saddens me to think that you dedicated so much of your life to helping others—the students whom you taught, the boys in your Sunday school class, the women in the Alpha Suffrage Club, and the poor southern men who migrated to Chicago in the early 1900s—but never experienced the joy of a close personal friendship. Calling you a "Lonely Warrior," Thomas C. Holt writes, perhaps too critically, of the rejection, isolation, and bitterness of your later years, brought on by your ideological differences and power struggles with Black leaders, particularly Booker T. Washington, at the turn of the century. The word "isolation" evoked the words with which you characterized yourself as a young woman:

I don't know what's the matter with me, I feel so dissatisfied with my life, so isolated from all my kind. I cannot or do not make friends & these fits of loneliness will come & I tire of everything. My life seems awry, the machinery out of gear & I feel there is something wrong.

Loneliness seems to run like a dark thread through the fabric of your life. Tragically, it was one of the demons that you could not exorcise.

And so, dear friend, I leave you with

Love,
Miriam

These letters reveal my complex and ambivalent feelings toward Ida B. Wells. In my last letter I have deliberately pulled back, distancing myself from her life and text, because I feel such strong emotions: relief that the project is over, joy that the diary is in print, empathy for a woman who suffered alienation and loneliness in her later years, and sadness over separation from someone whose life has touched mine in so many ways.

Whenever I recover a lost text like Wells's diary or examine the life of a forgotten pioneer like Dr. Georgia L. Patton or illuminate the work of a poet such as Nancy Morejón, I feel privileged, honored, chosen. I was pleased to learn from my editor at Beacon that the *Memphis Diary* has sold well, particularly because it was initially considered a somewhat "risky" project. I was even more gratified to discover that readers understand the enormous work that has gone into its production—the tedious research and constant revision, the hundreds of letters and piles of notes, the long hours and sleepless nights. Readers also understood the value of her diary "as a place where [Wells] might sort out her experiences, her emotions and her plans . . . [and could] disclose her intellectual restlessness and curiosity."

REPRESENTING TRUTH

Sojourner Truth's Knowing and Becoming Known

nell irvin painter

In New York City on the first of June, 1843, a woman known as Isabella Van Wagner changed her name to Sojourner Truth and began an itinerant ministry. The date was momentous, for in 1843, June 1 was Pentecost, the Christian holiday that falls fifty days after Easter and commemorates the day when the Holy Spirit filled Jesus' disciples and gave them the power to preach to strangers.[1]

Born into slavery in New York State, in the Hudson River county of Ulster, about 1797, Isabella took up her ministry in obedience to the Pentecostal imperative that had divided her life between slavery and freedom sixteen years before. The power of the Holy Spirit had struck her first in 1827, when emancipation in New York State, Pentecost, and the attendant slave holiday of Pinkster had virtually coincided. Isabella underwent a cataclysmic religious experience and the Holy Spirit, the power within Pentecost, remained a crucial force throughout her life—a source of inspiration and a means of

knowing. To the woman who became Sojourner Truth, knowing and being known were always of both material and episte-
mological significance.[2]

In this essay, posing questions that previous biographers of
Truth have ignored, I will examine how Sojourner Truth used
language—spoken and printed—as self-fashioning, and how
others, White women with more education and facility with
the culture of the printed word, portrayed her in published
phrases that became the kind of source material most congenial
to historians. My trajectory passes through nineteenth-century
information systems and some encounters related to the construction of the Sojourner Truth persona by other people, part
of the phenomenon that I call invented greats. I end with
the observation that words alone do not encompass Truth's
memory, for she used photography to embody and to empower
herself, to present the images of herself that *she* wanted remembered.[3] Working on Sojourner Truth has taught me that if we
are to write thoughtful biographies of people who were not
highly educated and who did not leave generous caches of personal papers in the archives where historians have traditionally
done their work, we will need to develop means of knowing our
subjects, and adapt to our subjects' ways of making themselves
known, that look beyond the written word.

Beginning on that day of Pentecost in 1843, when Sojourner
Truth, this daughter and servant, set out under a new name,
she reached many sorts of people, not strictly speaking in for-
eign tongues like the disciples, yet using various verbal and
visual means of communication, various languages, so to
speak. Over the course of her career as preacher, abolitionist,
and feminist, Truth (c. 1797–1883) used speech, writing, and
photography to convey her message and satisfy her material
needs. "Sojourner Truth," which translates as itinerant

preacher, described her calling rather than the occupation of household worker through which she gained her livelihood. This haunting new name expressed two of her three main preoccupations: transitoriness/permanence and distrust/credibility. As a working woman who had been born in slavery, she never became wealthy enough to take her means of subsistence for granted, and so money remained her third preoccupation.

With near literalness, the name "Truth" expresses her apprehension about trust. Isabella Van Wagner lived in a world full of people anxious to be believed, including the self-styled Prophet Matthias in whose Westchester County commune, called his "kingdom," she lived from 1832 to 1835.[4] Robert Matthews, who called himself "the Prophet Matthias" and "the Spirit of Truth" when he proselytized in New York City in the early 1830s, convinced Isabella and her co-religionists of his holiness. He gathered his followers around him in a kingdom that quickly disintegrated. By 1835 Matthews/Matthias had been chased out of New York City and gone west; by 1842 he had died.[5] The ideal of the spirit of truth lived on in his follower.

When Isabella became Sojourner Truth in 1843, she was not merely appropriating the cognomen of her erstwhile spiritual leader, for she had other, preexisting reasons for her own preoccupation with credibility. As a girl, she had been beaten and sexually abused, and as an enslaved worker, she had found her word doubted. In 1835 she overcame her usual reticence to persuade a New York freethinking journalist, Gilbert Vale, to present her story of the Matthias Kingdom. In a book whose subtitle ended *Containing the Whole Truth—and Nothing But the Truth*, Vale conveyed her desire to present "the *Truth*," "the *truth*," "the whole truth," "the *whole truth*."[6] In the 1820s, 1830s, and 1840s, when her concerns about being believed were recorded, she also went to court twice over matters of enormous familial and material importance. In 1828, in order to regain custody of her son Peter, illegally sold into slavery in Alabama, she had to convince a judge in Ulster County, New York, that she was her son's mother. Seven years later, in Westchester County, New York, she sued a couple for libel because they had charged her with poisoning, an accusation ruinous to someone who made her living by cooking for other people. In both court cases, Isabella prevailed, but the experiences surely reinforced her anxiety over the integrity of her word.[7]

As an abused child, oppressed worker, and litigant, she was liable to be doubted in situations of the utmost seriousness. Taken together, these three kinds of experience virtually overdetermined the choice of her new name. "Truth," her self-designation, raises a host of questions related to knowledge, representation, and communication, regarding what I call knowing and being known; those questions are the subject of this essay. I will leave "Sojourner," which speaks to another set of issues regarding impermanence, for another time.

SOJOURNER TRUTH'S KNOWING

Merely asking about the education of "Sojourner Truth" immediately raises the question of the identity of this complex figure. My full-length biography of Truth carries the subtitle *A Life, A Symbol* to accentuate, perhaps to exaggerate, the distinction between the symbolic figure Sojourner Truth, who stands for strong Black women, and the historical character Isabella, who was born a slave in the Hudson River valley of New York in about 1797 and who created "Sojourner Truth" at a specific historical juncture.[8]

In good twentieth-century fashion, Truth created a persona that filled a need in American political culture; both the culture and the need still exist today. The image of the mature Sojourner Truth, former slave and emblematic black feminist abolitionist, works metonymically as *the* Black woman in American history. The sturdy binary opposite of the debilitated, artificial White lady, Truth is appreciated as straight talking, authentic, unsentimental. She appears to be natural and spontaneous, and in the best tradition of famous Americans, she symbolizes a message worth noting.[9] Truth's persona demands that women who had been enslaved and whose children had been sold be included in the categories of "woman" and "the Negro."

As a symbol of race and gender, Sojourner Truth is usually summed up in a series of public speech acts, the most famous of which is "Ar'n't I a woman?," which Frances Dana Gage reported that Truth uttered at a woman's rights convention in Akron, Ohio, in 1851. This phrase is sometimes rendered more authentically Negro as "*Ain't* I a woman?" Truth is also known for baring her breast before a skeptical audience in Indiana in 1858. In the post-1960s, post–Black Power era of the late twentieth century, a fictive, hybrid cameo of these two actions presents an angry Sojourner Truth, who snarls, "And ain't I a woman?" then defiantly exhibits her breast.[10]

The metonymic Sojourner Truth has knowledge, but no education beyond her experience of slavery. She would seem to have acquired her knowledge in a figurative enslavement, which occurred in a no-time and a no-place located in an abstraction of the antebellum South, as opposed to the Hudson River valley of New York, where Isabella was actually enslaved. What the symbol of Sojourner Truth learned once and for all in slavery

enables her to analyze and challenge commonplaces of American race and gender thought. Having been a slave from 1797 to
1827, she needs no further instruction, for it could not affect
her opinions or her methods. Of itself, experiencing slavery—
not analyzing, representing, or making use of it—primed the
figurative Truth to demand, "Ar'n't I a woman?"

Within the figurative construction of Sojourner Truth, the
knowledge she took from slavery seems to reach late twentieth-
century audiences directly. It would seem that she spoke and
automatically entered historical memory permanently, so that
we still hear her a century and a quarter later through her own
originating force. She would seem to speak to us with a
potency that allows her words to endure just as she uttered
them, undistorted, unmediated, unedited, unchanging. This
Sojourner Truth would not take advantage of technology, nor
would she learn techniques of publicity from the people
around her. She would not need to learn any skills in order to
make herself appealing, for that would have been her
birthright. Women with access to print would immediately
have seen her as memorable, and they would have recorded her
transparently, powerless to shade the image that is now so
eagerly consumed. Both her knowledge of the way things were
and our knowledge of her would seem to be utterly natural and
unvarying. Or so it would seem.

Unlike the emblematic Sojourner Truth, the historical figure,
whom I am calling Isabella when I speak of her life before 1843,
had an education that began in slavery but did not end there.
Her first teacher was her mother, Elizabeth, who taught her to
say one of the two standard prayers of Christianity, the Pater
Noster or Lord's Prayer. From her parents Isabella also learned
her family's history of loss through the slave trade that scat-

tered children throughout the North and conveyed thousands of Black New Yorkers into perpetual slavery in the South. She was conscious of being a survivor until she reached the age of ten, when her turn to be sold came. Her parents also would have taught her appropriate behavior through corporal punishment, and as a parent she provided the same sort of education by beating her own children.[11]

It was not illegal in New York State to teach slaves to read and write when Isabella was a child, and from the late eighteenth century until slavery was abolished in New York in 1827, a few very fortunate slaves managed to attend missionary schools. The schools, which were located in New York City or other towns such as Albany, lay well beyond Isabella's reach.[12] As a rural person and as a girl, Isabella never went to school. Neither as a child nor as an adult did she ever learn to read or write.

After her emancipation, several people tried to tutor her, for like late twentieth-century people, educated nineteenth-century people took literacy as the signifier of modernity and saw reading as the best means of acquiring knowledge.[13] Then, as now, an inability to read and write seemed the same as ignorance, although often this was not the case. Without direct access to the written word, Isabella/Truth nonetheless used reading along with other means of gathering information. Her ways were those of people who are deeply religious, rural, female, poor, or unschooled. All these categories included Americans who were Black and/or unfree, but the correlations were not automatic, as the dissimilar pursuits of Frederick Douglass and Sojourner Truth confirm.

In the mid-1840s, Frederick Douglass and Sojourner Truth, two former slaves of contrasting temperament, got to know each other in the Northampton Association of Education and

Industry in Northampton, Massachusetts, a utopian community, founded in 1841, that engaged in the cooperative production of silk. Douglass, who had escaped from slavery in Maryland in 1838 and become a protégé of William Lloyd Garrison, was teaching himself, in his words, "to speak and act like a person of cultivation and refinement"—an effort in which he succeeded brilliantly. Douglass, like many other fugitive slaves, associated illiteracy with enslavement and strove to complete his emancipation through the acquisition of fluency—elegance, to be more precise—in reading and writing. Marking his distance from Truth, Douglass recalled her as a "strange compound of wit and wisdom, of wild enthusiasm and flintlike common sense. She was a genuine specimen of the uncultured [N]egro. She cared very little for elegance of speech or refinement of manners." While Douglass was trying to acquire the polish of a modern educated man, Truth, he said, "seemed to feel it her duty to trip me up in my speeches and to ridicule [me]." Literacy was the main means Douglass used as he sought to establish himself as a free person, but Truth appeared to disdain the print-based culture he was mastering. She did not need to read in order to know.[14]

From the 1830s until her death, observers commented upon her intelligence. According to Gilbert Vale, the free-thought journalist who came to know Truth in the mid-1830s, she had "a peculiar and marked character. Nature has furnished her, not with a beautiful, but with a strong body and mind." He described her as "not exactly bad looking but there is nothing prepossessing or very observant or intelligent in her looks." After long conversations with her, he found her to be a woman of "shrewd, common sense, energetic manners . . . [who] apparently despises artifice," but he inserted a caveat: She was "not exactly what she seems." She was quiet and reflective and had her own private and very wise opinions about everything and everybody. Ever the keen observer, she usually kept those opinions to herself. In 1851, while she was still obscure, Rochester, New York, abolitionists noticed her perspicacity. One warned, "If any one wants to play a bo-peep game with truth, beware of Sojourner," for although she seems "simple and artless . . . her eye will see your heart and apprehend your motives, almost like God's." Another concluded that Truth's illiteracy was "the shield to guard her rare intuitions, her great pure heart and strong individuality from any worldly taint." Obviously, illiteracy did not separate Truth from wisdom.[15]

Isabella/Sojourner Truth employed three main ways of knowing: observation and practice, divine inspiration, and, in a special sense of the word, reading. In none was she unique. First, as the New York journalist recognized in the 1830s, she was a shrewd observer of other people. As a slave, a woman, a Black person, and a household worker, Isabella learned to decipher other people as a technique for survival. Once called woman's intuition, this ability to decode others without indicating what one perceives is a sense cultivated by the powerless who seek to survive their encounters with the powerful. Isabella occupied a subaltern subject position, and she kept her eyes open and her mouth closed unless she was in a protected situation or had some pressing motive for speaking out.

Isabella learned the skills she used as a worker and a speaker through apprenticeship and practice, as nonreaders have done over the ages, and as readers still do when faced with difficult maneuvers that are hard to convey in writing. As a free woman in New York City, Isabella worked in the households of the same people over many years; that record is testimony to her competence in performing to a metropolitan standard. These household skills served Truth in her subsequent career. When

she first went on the road as a preacher in 1843, she earned
subsistence and respect by cooking dishes à la New York City
for provincials on Long Island. This knowledge proved useful
again in the late 1860s, when she was employed as the matron
at the Freedmen's Village in Washington, D.C., and taught
freedwomen the very same household skills.

As a preacher, Sojourner Truth learned through rehearsal.
Even before she left the Hudson River valley, her employer's
brother reported that she worked in the kitchen "preaching as
she went and kept preaching all day." Her employer "told her
she ought to live somewhere in a big place where she would
have a good many people to preach to." In the late 1820s and
early 1830s, she preached regularly at the camp meetings that
convened around New York City, where she became very popular.[16] By the time she joined the antislavery feminist lecture circuit in the late 1840s, Sojourner Truth was a practiced public
speaker. She had long since conquered stage fright and doubts
about the propriety of speaking in large, mixed gatherings
when she stood up to speak to reformers.

Like many people who are very religious, Isabella / Truth
learned through a second channel, divine inspiration—the
voice of the Holy Spirit—a route to knowledge through faith
that many believers, then and now, prefer to formal education.
Pentecostals such as Truth prize the voice of the Holy Spirit as
the premier means of enlightenment.

Sojourner Truth said that she talked to God, and God
talked to her. Truth may have distrusted writing, as people bred
in oral cultures have over the centuries.[17]

Isabella/Sojourner Truth did use writing and printing, both
as a third means of learning and as a way of communicating
with others. What Truth learned from written texts, especially
the Bible, came not through the solitary study that academics

practice, not through seeing words and reading them silently, but in the traditional manner, through listening to someone read writing aloud. In hearing the Bible, Truth studied it. Analysts of reading and literacy emphasize that her way of using writing has been far more prevalent over the course of human history than literate people acknowledge. She was one of the masses of early nineteenth-century evangelical Protestants who believed that scholarly commentary, indeed, any commentary, obscured the deeper meaning of the Bible, which spoke directly to each believer. She preferred children to adults as readers, she said, because children would read the same passage repeatedly, without interpretation, whereas adults tended to lapse into useless explanation when asked to repeat a verse.[18]

In a system of spoken knowledge, authorship is a more complex matter than when thinker and scribe are one, for the functions of author and writer are disconnected. The author of the text is the knower and speaker, while the person who writes down the words is the amanuensis. Sojourner Truth used writing in this way when she dictated her autobiography to Olive Gilbert in Northampton in the late 1840s. Gilbert interposed her own ear and by dint of having taken down a third-person narrative acquired citation as the author of the *Narrative of Sojourner Truth.*

Bibliographical citation encourages the contrast between Olive Gilbert, the educated manipulator of the pen, and Sojourner Truth, the narrator untouched by literate culture, but such a dichotomy separates their roles too neatly. (As Gayatri Chakravorty Spivak would say, so stark a contrast saturates their identities.) Only the symbolic figure of Sojourner Truth could preserve an uncontaminated ignorance of the power of printed narration after having lived around educated people for decades. The historical person Isabella / Truth was an employee and comrade of wealthy and educated people in New York City, the Matthias commune, and the Northampton Association in the 1830s and 1840s. Though she may have poked fun at young Frederick Douglass, she, like him, absorbed the ideals and practices of people who were more firmly implanted in the metropolitan culture of writing and respectability. One telltale sign is a criticism of her peers in slavery in rural Ulster County: their thoughts, she says in her *Narrative*, were no longer than her little finger. Her photographs (to which I shall return) similarly betray an acceptance of the material culture of the people with whom she lived.[19]

In addition to her narrative, Truth occasionally dictated letters to friends and associates, of which few are extant. Those that survive deal with commodities, with the selling and distributing of her material means of support: her books and photographs. She was looking to sell and promote her narrative when she encountered two of the educated White women who made her widely known in the nineteenth and twentieth centuries: Harriet Beecher Stowe and Frances Dana Gage. Gage, especially, was keenly sensitive to women's disadvantages vis-à-vis men in American political culture. But compared with Truth, she possessed enormous power within the information network in which they both functioned, and her ability to shape perceptions of Truth far outstripped Truth's own, at least through print. Truth had a magnetic personality, but she was not formally educated, and only through others could she communicate in writing. Hence the meanings of her persona were more subject to other people's interpretation than is usual when a literate person moves onto the public stage.[20] The disjuncture between self-representation and Truth's representation at the hands of others creates unexpected complications for a biographer trained as an academic historian, for the memory of Truth resides in words that do not render their meaning straightforwardly and in images that we historians are not trained to interpret. Coming to know Sojourner Truth requires familiarity with more than our everyday printed words.

KNOWING SOJOURNER TRUTH

The first thing that strikes a historical biographer of Sojourner Truth is an embarrassment in regard to the rhetorical question "Ar'n't I a woman?," for which she is famous. A look in volume 4 of the *Black Abolitionists' Papers* shows that, although Truth gave a speech in the famous venue, Akron, Ohio, in the famous year, 1851, the contemporary report does not include the crucial line. Before the *Black Abolitionists' Papers* went to press, the editor and staff passionately debated which version of the speech to publish. Ultimately, they followed their regular editorial policies and published the report of Truth's speech that had appeared in the *Salem* [Ohio] *Anti-Slavery Bugle* in June 1851. According to C. Peter Ripley, editor of the Black Abolitionist Papers Project, it was "the most complete and accurate version" of the event. Further, he adds, the circumstances surrounding the *Bugle*'s report—its contemporaneity, its author's familiarity with Truth—reinforced its reliability.[21]

The second thing that strikes a biographer seeking to pierce the mystery of Sojourner Truth's 1851 speech is that other documentation is not to be found where historians normally look. This is true of women's history in general, as Virginia Woolf noted in 1929 in *A Room of One's Own*. There she asks, rhetorically, of research on women: "If truth is not to be found on the shelves of the British Museum, where is . . . truth?[22] No, Truth is not in the British Museum or in other archives; her sources are mostly periodical reports of her speeches, many of which she gave to encourage sales of the objects that she sold to support herself, themselves valuable sources. These are her *Narrative* and photographic portraits ("shadows") that she paid for and therefore controlled. The answer to the question of how Truth and "Ar'n't I a woman?" became identified lies in what might be termed Sojourner Truth's marketing technique.

Sojourner Truth, the itinerant preacher, created and marketed the persona of a charismatic woman who had been a slave, and it is precisely through her marketing of herself or, as she put it, her selling the shadow to support her substance, that her name is known today. As the principal symbol of strength and Blackness in the iconography of women's culture, Truth has been bought and sold for more than a century. She had dozens of colleagues among feminist abolitionists, such as Frances Dana Gage, and itinerant preachers, such as Harriet Livermore, whose names have been almost totally forgotten. Truth's Black female peers—the abolitionists Maria Stewart, Sarah Douglass, Sarah Remond, and Frances Ellen Watkins Harper and the preachers Jarena Lee, Zilpha Elaw, Julia Foote, and Rebecca Cox Jackson—are just as obscure.

The difference is that Truth, though illiterate, utilized the information systems of her time with phenomenal success. To recover her traces, a biographer must consult her preferred, visual medium of photography, as well as the biographer's own, which is language in print. What is known of Sojourner Truth in print comes mainly from the pens of four educated White women (Olive Gilbert, Harriet Beecher Stowe, Frances Dana Gage, and Frances Titus) who were fascinated by Truth and sought to capture her in writing. Titus, who was Truth's neighbor and publicist in Battle Creek, Michigan, accompanied Truth on speaking trips in the 1870s and arranged for the republication of her *Narrative* in the 1870s and 1880s. There Titus listed herself as author.[23] Titus's work has a place in a comprehensive analysis of the making of the figure of Sojourner Truth, but by the time she joined Truth's enterprise, the persona and the epistemology of Sojourner Truth had already taken shape.

Narratives of Sojourner Truth

The first of Truth's amanuenses was Olive Gilbert, to whom Truth dictated her life story, which Truth published in 1850 in Boston as the *Narrative of Sojourner Truth*. This 128-page pamphlet narrates Isabella's life as a slave, her conversion in 1827, and her experiences with New York Pentecostals (then called Perfectionists), including her time in the kingdom of the Prophet Matthias. The *Narrative* ends on a pathetic note, with Truth disillusioned by her experiences in intentional communities: the Matthias Kingdom and the Northampton Association. In a tone innocent of bitterness or anger, she expresses satisfaction that her old owner, John J. Dumont, has come to see the evil inherent in slavery. Truth emerges from the first edition of her *Narrative* as a slightly piteous figure, an object of charity whose life story is first and foremost for sale. That tale is bound to disappoint anyone seeking the powerful feminist abolitionist of the 1850s or the dignified figure of the photographs from the 1860s and 1870s.

When Sojourner Truth and Olive Gilbert collaborated on the manuscript that would become the *Narrative*, both were resident in the Northampton Association of Education and Industry. Truth had arrived at Northampton in the late fall of 1843, after her first half year as "Sojourner Truth." Olive Gilbert belonged to the Northampton Association in 1845 and 1846.[24]

Little is known of Gilbert: She was born in 1801 and was from Brooklyn, Connecticut. Relatively well educated and well read, Gilbert was of a utopian and spiritualist turn of mind. She spent almost two years between 1846 and 1849 in Daviess County in northern Kentucky, probably as a governess, which interrupted her work with Truth. After stints back in her Connecticut hometown at midcentury, Gilbert returned to Leeds, in the Northampton environs, and she still belonged to reform-minded circles in the early 1870s.[25]

Americans with antislavery and feminist convictions seem to have been unusually predisposed to purchase information conveyed in print. Reflecting this predilection, the ex-slave narrative as a genre came of age in the 1840s. Slave narratives had appeared since 1760, but in the 1840s several—by Frederick Douglass, William Wells Brown, and Henry Bibb—became best-sellers. The "great enabling text" was the *Narrative of the Life of Frederick Douglass, An American Slave*, which appeared in 1845 and sold forty-five hundred copies in less than six months. It was reprinted six times in four years.[26] As a publishing phenomenon and as the autobiography of a man whom Truth had encountered at the Northampton Association, the *Narrative of the Life of Frederick Douglass* would have inspired Sojourner Truth. The genesis of the project that became the *Narrative of Sojourner Truth* is unclear, but the mid-1840s were auspicious culturally and technologically.

After Gilbert and Truth completed their work in 1849, Truth's Northampton connections paid off again, this time through her contact with William Lloyd Garrison, the editor of the Boston-based *Liberator*. Garrison's American Anti-Slavery Society had published Douglass's narrative, and both Garrison and Douglass treated the Northampton Association as a sort of progressive summer camp. Garrison had family there, for he had married the sister of George Benson, one of the association's founders. Through Benson and Garrison, Truth contacted George Brown Yerrinton, the printer of the *Liberator*, a freethinker whose ties to progressive causes and publications dated back to the 1820s. Thus the Northampton Association not only helped Truth ease herself out of preaching and into antislavery and woman's rights advocacy, it also located her printer.[27]

From an otherwise unknown James Boyle, Truth obtained the money to have her *Narrative* printed.[28] Because Truth paid for the printing, Yerrinton cannot be called the publisher of her book, though he later sold her the stereotyped plates. That Truth published herself was not unusual at the time, for the line between publisher and printer was only becoming established in the 1850s, and the functions of printing, distributing, and selling books were not always distinct. Sojourner Truth, acting as her own distributor and bookseller, was well within the bounds of ordinary practice. What was unusual was the book's price, kept low, perhaps, to facilitate purchase. At twenty-five cents per copy, her 128-page, 7¾-by-5-inch, soft-covered *Narrative* represented a bargain.

Sojourner Truth's *Narrative*, which is seldom cited as a source of information on slavery in New York or in general, seems to have been appreciated by its purchasers more as an object than as a text. Any book straddles the blurry boundary between text and object, but Truth's *Narrative* is particularly difficult to classify. It is the autobiography of a woman who neither read nor wrote, and it was made to provide her material support. The *Narrative* seems to have been little read—it was not discussed as a text, and it may have represented less a text that conveyed meaning than an artifact, a commodity. As a work composed to raise money, Truth's *Narrative* belonged to a recognizable subgenre of Black autobiography.[29] In this regard, it resembled the tokens that recipients of charity still offer to givers. Well-intentioned reformers went to hear Sojourner Truth present herself as a slave mother and bought copies of her little book to express solidarity, to contribute to her well-being, and to indicate their own relative position and status in society. As Truth sold her being as a slave woman, her customers bought the proof of their social difference from her.[30]

More than a century and a quarter after its publication, the *Narrative of Sojourner Truth* still has not found its niche in the literature of ex-slaves. Although Truth's images often figure as symbols of Black womanhood, she is never discussed as a slave narrator and her account is rarely quarried for information on enslaved Blacks in New York State. Compared with Douglass's three autobiographies—particularly the first, which has continually been republished in popular editions—Truth's *Narrative* until recently remained expensive and inaccessible.[31]

Truth's strategy for publicizing her book and increasing its sales has served authors for centuries. Like authors then and now, Truth went on the lecture circuit after she published her book in 1850, speaking and selling copies to audiences who were intrigued by her personal appearance. Among the meetings she attended to sell her book was the 1851 woman's rights convention in Akron.

Personal appearances worked well in the market that Truth could reach personally, but her obscurity militated against her with people she could not address. To communicate with a broader range of potential buyers, she needed the endorsement of those better known than she. Although Garrison had introduced the first edition of her book in 1850, authenticating her standing as an ex-slave and attesting to the virtue of the purchase, in 1853 Truth seized the initiative when she realized that a profitable endorsement was within her reach. Joining the legions of authors and publishers seeking advantageous "puffs"—now called blurbs—Truth approached the world's best-selling author for a puff, which she received. It began:

> The following narrative may be relied upon as in all respects true & faithful, & it is in some points more remarkable & interesting than many narratives of the kind which have abounded in late years.
>
> It is the history of a mind of no common energy & power whose struggles with the darkness & ignorance of slavery have a peculiar interest. The truths of Christianity seem to have come to her almost by a separate revelation & seem to verify the beautiful words of scripture "I will bring the blind by a way that they knew not, I will make darkness light before them & crooked things straight."

There is no way of knowing whether Stowe's puff boosted Truth's sales, but it certainly began a discursive relationship between Sojourner Truth and Harriet Beecher Stowe that extended into the following decade.[32]

The 1851 publication of *Uncle Tom's Cabin* as a serial in Gamaliel Bailey's moderate, antislavery Washington *National Era* had proved wildly successful, and when the book appeared in 1852, it became a sensation that transformed its author's career. Stowe had been writing since the mid-1830s, but the shocking revision of the Fugitive Slave Act in the Compromise of 1850 galvanized her into writing the book that broke records throughout the world. The first year's sales of *Uncle Tom's Cabin* reached a phenomenal three hundred thousand, bringing Stowe ten thousand dollars in royalties, a fortune at the time.[33]

Uncle Tom's Cabin made Stowe a highly sought-after author. In 1863, ten years after Sojourner Truth had come soliciting a blurb, Stowe reworked a short piece she had written in 1860 and published it in the *Atlantic Monthly* as "Sojourner Truth, the Libyan Sibyl."[34]

Having adjusted her lifestyle to a prosperity that could be maintained only by a constant influx of additional funds, Stowe was writing quickly about a marketable subject.[35] She had never been a radical abolitionist—and she was only a moderate advocate of woman's rights—but in the early 1860s material on the Negro was very much in demand. With the Emancipation Proclamation and the acceptance of Black men into the Union army, northern newspapers and magazines were full of articles on Blacks. Writing to the market, Stowe presented a tableau in which she and her family appeared as people of culture who appreciated Sojourner Truth as a primitive *objet d'art* and source of entertainment. In her use of the name *sibyl*, Stowe captured Truth's prophetic side. Above all, however, Stowe emphasized Truth's Africanness and otherness, tendering her speech in Negro dialect and praising her naïveté. Mining the vein that had produced her Black characters in *Uncle Tom's Cabin*, Stowe made Truth into a quaint and innocent exotic who disdained feminism.

Stowe presents Truth as telling of becoming a Methodist in Ulster County in about 1827. The quote, in dialect, is framed by Stowe's comments, in standard English. Stowe quotes herself as asking: "But, Sojourner, had you never been told about Jesus Christ?" To which Truth answers:

No, honey. I had n't heerd no preachin'—been to no meetin'. Nobody had n't told me. I'd kind o' heerd of Jesus, but thought he was like Gineral Lafayette, or some o' them. But one night there was a Methodist meetin' somewhere in our parts, an' I went; an' they got up an' begun for to tell der'speriences: an' de fust one begun to speak. I started, 'cause he told about Jesus. . . . An' finally I said, "Why they all know him!" I was so happy! an' then they sung this hymn.

Stowe then adds, again in contrasting standard English: "(Here Sojourner sang, in a strange, cracked voice, but evidently with all her soul and might, mispronouncing the English, but seeming to derive as much elevation and comfort from bad English as from good)." After quoting Truth's hymn, "There Is a Holy City," Stowe explains that Truth "sang with the strong barbaric accent of the native African . . . Sojourner, singing this hymn, seemed to impersonate the fervor of Ethiopia, wild, savage, hunted of all nations, but burning after God in her tropic heart."[36]

In "Sojourner Truth, the Libyan Sibyl," Stowe made mistakes, some careless, some contrived: She wrote, for instance, that Truth had come from Africa, and, even though Truth was very much alive and active in Washington, D.C., at the time, that she was dead. (Truth did not die until 1883.) For all her misstatements, Stowe provided Truth with the identity that would cling to her until late in the nineteenth century.

A more obscure person who was still in the thick of the woman's rights and antislavery movements might well be chagrined by Stowe's commercialism, particularly if there was an element of rivalry. Stowe's article thus roused another woman writer with far stronger reform credentials, Frances Dana Gage, to write.

. . .

An Ohio radical, Frances Dana Gage (1808–1884) was known
as a woman's rights woman whose writing appeared occasionally in the *Independent*. Largely self-educated, Gage contributed to feminist and agricultural newspapers in the 1850s
and 1860s under the pen name Aunt Fanny and became a popular public speaker. She corresponded familiarly with Susan B.
Anthony, with whom she toured in 1856.[37] As an antislavery
feminist, Gage was both a sharp critic of the patriarchal family
and a folksy character who wrapped her critique of conventional society in the commonplaces of her role as wife and
mother of eight. Although recognized as a talented speaker
and writer within temperance, antislavery, and feminist circles,
Gage never took the step up to the *Atlantic Monthly* or other
widely read, fashionable magazines. Throughout her life she
remained with the religious and feminist press, and among her
eleven books of fiction, those published for temperance organizations predominate.

Gage was unusual, though not unique, in focusing her
woman's rights rhetoric on working-class women. When
antifeminists protested that equal rights would expose women
to the rough-and-tumble of economic and political strife,
Gage pointed to poor women who were already immersed in an
acute struggle for existence, working as hard as men in thor-
oughly unpleasant circumstances but handicapped by their
lack of civil rights and equal pay.

Gage had chaired the 1851 woman's rights convention in
Akron where Truth had come to sell her newly published *Narrative*. She did not write an essay dedicated entirely to Truth
immediately, but Gage recognized the attractiveness of Truth's
persona and used her as the model for an October 1851

episode of a series she was publishing in Jane Swisshelm's *Pitts-burgh Saturday Visiter.*[38]

Less than a month after the appearance of Stowe's "Libyan Sibyl," Gage published in the *Independent* the account of Truth that we recognize today. Gage quoted Sojourner Truth as saying that she had had thirteen children, all of whom had been sold away from her (although Truth had five children and said so in her *Narrative*). In this letter these famous lines appeared for the first time: "And ar'n't I a woman? Look at me. Look at my arm. . . . I have plowed and planted and gathered into barns, and no man could head me—and ar'n't I a woman?"[39]

Stowe and Gage let many years intervene between meeting Truth and writing about her by name. But while Stowe drew Truth as a quaint, minstrel-like, nineteenth-century Negro, Gage made her into a tough-minded, feminist emblem by stressing Truth's strength and the clash of conventions of race and gender and by inventing the riveting refrain, "And ar'n't I a woman?" During the mid-nineteenth century, Stowe's rendition of Truth captured American imaginations, and the phrase "Libyan Sibyl" was endlessly reworked, even by Gage, who termed Truth the "Libyan Statue" in her letter to the *Independent*, and Olive Gilbert, who in a letter to Truth written in the 1870s spoke of Truth as the "American Sibyl."[40]

Along with another phrase that had appeared in Stowe's piece—Truth's rhetorical and possibly apocryphal question to Douglass, "Frederick, is God dead?"—versions of the "Libyan Sibyl" personified Truth until the end of the nineteenth century.[41] As an expression of enduring Christian faith, she became the authentic Negro woman, the native, the genius of spiritual inspiration uncorrupted by formal education. Toward the end of the century, however, Gage's version of Truth began to overtake Stowe's, as woman suffragists advanced Gage's Truth.

Although Frances Titus had reprinted Gage's letter as well as Stowe's article in the 1878 edition of *The Narrative of Sojourner Truth*, the primary means of popularizing "And ar'n't I a woman?" was the publication of the *History of Woman Suffrage* in 1881.[42] As for the antislavery movement, so for woman suffrage: Those nineteenth-century Americans who were attuned to the power of the published record have profoundly influenced subsequent representations of the past. Nineteenth-century evangelicals outside the mainline denominations—who were far more likely to hear, comprehend, and appreciate Sojourner Truth in her own self-definition as a preacher—were less solicitous than reformers about preserving and publishing their records. Practically by default, the feminists and abolitionists, who published copiously, fashioned the historic Sojourner Truth in their own image, the one created by the feminist Frances Dana Gage.

As the woman suffrage pioneers Susan B. Anthony and Elizabeth Cady Stanton were growing old in the late 1870s, they recognized a need to gather and publish the papers of the movement they had inspired in 1848 and organized in the succeeding thirty years. They wrote surviving activists to request documents, which they combined with newspaper reports and published in three volumes between 1881 and 1886. Stanton was living in Tenafly, in northern New Jersey, as she carried out most of the work; Anthony came from Rochester, New York, from time to time to visit and assist. Gage, who in the years since 1851 had moved from McConnellsville, Ohio, to St. Louis, was then living in Vineland, in southern New Jersey, a center of temperance and woman's rights enthusiasm. Having corresponded with Anthony and Stanton since the 1850s, Gage would have welcomed a request to contribute material for the *History of Woman Suffrage*. In 1879 she wrote that she was looking over her old papers and manuscripts.[43]

The feminist press of the 1880s testifies to Gage's enduring reputation as an ardent feminist. Although in wretched health, she continued to contribute to women's newspapers. After Sojourner Truth's death in 1883, the *Boston Woman's Journal* reprinted Gage's report of Truth's Akron speech. Through letters to feminist gatherings and published utterances, Gage spoke for temperance and woman suffrage right up to her death in 1884.[44] Stowe, in contrast, had turned away from reform entirely.

By the end of the century, Gage's Truth was doing feminist work for woman suffragists all around the country, though sometimes in turn-of-the-century fashion. A Memphis suffragist who imagined Truth as an "old negro mammy" nevertheless quoted Gage's report of the 1851 speech as a stick with which to beat antisuffragists, in this instance, the Reverend Thomas Dixon.[45] No longer the symbol of Christian trust, the uncorrupted Negro, or African genius, Truth was now the embodiment of women's strength that Gage had crafted. Stowe's 1863 portrait of Truth, written by a best-selling author whose religious sensibility was stronger than her feminism, expressed Victorian sentimentality. Gage's 1863 portrait of Truth, written by a woman whose radicalism had kept her at the far margins of American letters during her lifetime, has worn—and sold— well during the twentieth century.

Invention and History

It may seem ironic that Sojourner Truth is known for words she did not say, but American history is full of symbols that do their work without a basis in life. As a Black and feminist talisman rather than a text, Sojourner Truth is still selling. She remains more sign than lived existence, like Betsy Ross, Chief Seattle, and Mason ("Parson") Weems's George Washington, who are also best remembered for deeds they did not perform and words they did not utter. Like other invented greats, Truth is consumed as a signifier and beloved for what we need her to have said. It is no accident that other people writing well after the fact made up what we see as most meaningful about each of those greats.

Today Americans who love Sojourner Truth cherish her for what they need her to have said and buy her images to invest in the idea of strong women, whether or not they are Black. As in the nineteenth century, Americans consume Sojourner Truth as the embodiment of a meaning necessary for their own cultural formations, even though that meaning has changed radically since Harriet Beecher Stowe first presented it. The market for historical symbols is not limited to words, however, and Sojourner Truth images, now distributed mostly through outlets catering to feminists, have also sold briskly. This is as it was in the mid-nineteenth century.

As a person whose depiction in print depended upon the imagination of other people, Sojourner Truth was able to influence those representations only marginally. Although she never distanced herself from the texts through which Gilbert and Gage portrayed her, she attempted to correct Stowe's article within three months of its publication, protesting in a letter to the *Boston Commonwealth* that she was not African and that she never called people "Honey." She sent the editor, James Redpath, six copies of her *Narrative*, suggesting that her correct history was to be between its covers. She also asked readers to purchase her photograph, for she was in ill health and restricted to her home in Battle Creek, Michigan. "I am," she said, "living on my shadow."[46] As though surrendering language to women who were initiated into the esoteric practices of writing and publishing, she sought self-representation in a medium that many Americans, even the highly educated, regarded as transparent and whose etymology came from the Greek words meaning "light writing": photography.

Truth in Photography

After the Stowe and Gage essays increased her visibility in 1863, Sojourner Truth found a new means of reaching supporters and raising money in the rage for the new *cartes de visite* from France. Between 1863 and about 1875, Sojourner Truth had at least fourteen photographic portraits made of herself in two formats, *carte de visite* (4 by 2½ inches) and cabinet card (6½ by 4½ inches), in at least seven sittings. In the 1860s and 1870s, Truth stocked copies of these photographs and the *Narrative of Sojourner Truth* to sell through the mail and wherever she made personal appearances. While donations of any size were welcome, Truth seems to have asked about $.33 for each *carte de visite* and $.50 for the larger cabinet cards, in line with the prices that photographers and publishers charged in the early 1860s, $2.00 to $3.00 per dozen.[47]

During the Civil War, *cartes de visite* filled a multitude of purposes. *Cartes de visite* of great men were sold as inspiration to the masses; authors (such as Stowe), politicians (such as Abraham Lincoln, whose 1860 *carte* by Mathew Brady was a campaign token), actors, and lecturers (such as Gage) carried them about and sold them at personal appearances and through other outlets as handy forms of publicity, like twentieth-century baseball cards. More to the point for Sojourner Truth, some circulated within the Union as anti-Confederate propaganda-images of starved prisoners of war from the Confederate prison at Andersonville, Georgia, the scourged back of the fugitive slave volunteer Gordon, and White-looking children whose Whiteness had not protected them from enslavement.[48] These fund-raising *cartes* may well have inspired Truth, for her portraits would also have served to remind purchasers that she symbolized the woman who had been a slave.

Had Truth's *cartes de visite* served only as abolitionist fund raising, Truth might have chosen to pose in settings or costumes that evoked the tragedy of her origins. Like Gordon of the whip-scarred back, she might have prominently exhibited some image of suffering or toil, such as her right hand, injured during her last year in slavery. Or she might have circulated the only image of Sojourner Truth other than her photographs (or engravings made from them), a sketch made of her in Northampton, probably in the 1860s. In this drawing, she is doing laundry, her arms plunged deep into wash water. That was not the kind of image in her photographs, and she did the choosing.[49]

The portrait, one of her favorites, was taken in Detroit in 1864. This *carte de visite* is in the vernacular style that became widespread in the 1850s, as daguerreotypes grew more popular than painted portraits with elaborate backdrops. This photo shows no landscape or interior, and the props—knitting, a book, and a vase full of flowers on a table—are simplified into tokens of leisure and feminine gentility. As in all of the other photographs of Sojourner Truth, she wears expertly tailored clothing made of handsome, substantial material, the black and white she favored for public speaking. In several portraits she is dressed in the Quaker-style clothing that feminist and antislavery lecturers wore to distinguish themselves from showily dressed actresses, who were not respectable figures. Her hair is wrapped plainly, but not in the madras handkerchief that Harriet Beecher Stowe characterized as in the "manner of her race."[50] In other photographs, Truth wears fashionable clothing, again very well tailored, and she presents the image of a respectable, middle-class matron but, perhaps, also that of a woman advertising her suitability as a model of civilized comportment for the freedwomen refugees in Washington, D.C.

She is sitting in a studio (in other portraits, also taken in studios, she stands with a cane or sits holding a book or portrait), with knitting in her hands and a book on the table. Truth knitted, but this yarn, held in only one hand, conveys mainly the motherliness that was central to her self-fashioning. According to the conventions of the genre of celebrity portraiture, she looks past the camera, which lends an air of weighty seriousness.[51] Her posture is relaxed but upright, communicating an impression of easy composure. For a woman of at least sixty-five, she looks remarkably young, but the relative youthfulness of her appearance takes nothing from the overall gravity of the persona. She is mature and intelligent, not reading, but wearing eyeglasses that might have helped her knit and that certainly, like the book on the table, gave her an educated air. In none of these portraits is there anything beyond Blackness that would inspire charity, nothing of the piteous slave mother, chest-baring insolent, grinning minstrel, or amusing naïf.

The original caption, "I Sell the Shadow to Support the Substance. SOJOURNER TRUTH," explains the photograph's fundraising function and is as much a part of the rhetoric of the image as the portrait itself. That caption rarely appears in late twentieth-century representations, although the image is for sale today from several feminist mail-order houses. Sojourner Truth photographs still bear a caption; however, sentences from Gage's "Ar'n't I a woman?" report replace "I sell the shadow to support the substance," because the market has changed, in its tastes and in its relation to Truth herself. Current consumers purchase images of Truth to embody strength, not dependence, no matter how dignified its composition. More to the point, it is no longer possible to contribute to Truth through purchase of her book or *carte de visite*. "I sell the shadow to support the substance" exhorted its original purchasers and today remains authentic, but in today's context, with Truth long dead and without heirs who claim her estate, it means very little.[52]

Like legions of other *cartes de visite*, Sojourner Truth's portraits show a solid bourgeoise, even to the eyeglasses. The image does not capture the woman who belonged to the weird Matthias Kingdom in the 1830s or who reportedly rolled up her sleeve to bare her arm or took down her bodice to show her breast in the 1850s. The woman sitting here does not look as though she would speak in dialect, and hers is the antithesis of a naked body. Blackness, of course, conveyed its own messages.

Even as her *cartes de visite* portrayed Sojourner Truth—the woman who had been a slave, the subject of the *Narrative of Sojourner Truth*, the advocate of Black emancipation and woman's rights—they also appealed to the preconditioned sight of her clientele, which transformed the palm-sized image of a woman in a studio into the simulacrum of a well-dressed Victorian in a tasteful parlor. These inherently discrepant meanings, like the tongues in which Jesus' disciples spoke to the people of many nations when the Holy Spirit filled them, were subject to reinterpretation. Photography may be writing with light, but like writing with words, it is a sign system and has its own rhetorics of representation.[53] Sojourner Truth was seizing control of her replicas: shaping the meaning of the images that she sold by deciding when to have her photograph taken, what to wear, what expression to adopt, which props to hold, and which photographer to patronize, while her photographer adjusted the framing, focus, and distance. Because she sold her *cartes de visite* to people whose possessions were likely to end up in repositories, she still exercises that control.

Sojourner Truth's photographic portraits are not transparent representations of her authentic being, nor do they convey a simple truth. In her *cartes de visite*, as in other photographs, the sense of reality is enigmatic. As one critic notes, photographic images are a place of "resistance to meaning."[54] If there is no unmediated access to Sojourner Truth, no means of knowing her with certainty, nonetheless some conclusions can be drawn about how she wanted to be known.

Sojourner Truth was willing to use the resources offered by popular culture to replicate and distribute representations of herself for her material support, and she did need the money. A slave until she was thirty, Isabella was destitute when she entered life as a free woman in 1827. She worked at ill-paid household labor in New York City until she became Sojourner Truth in 1843. Yet after the 1850 publication of her *Narrative*, she managed to buy a house in Northampton in 1850, a house in Harmonia, Michigan, in 1856, and a house in Battle Creek, Michigan, in the 1860s, in which she died in 1883. With the exception of $390 that the Freedmen's Bureau paid her for relief work in Washington after the Civil War, her means of support were the proceeds from the sale of her book and her "shadows" and donations from her reform-minded audiences and supporters. Considering the poverty in which masses of freed people and working women remained in the nineteenth century, her persona—as embodied in these objects—proved remunerative. By contrast, her husband had died in an Ulster County, New York, poorhouse before the Civil War, and her daughters died destitute in Battle Creek in the late nineteenth and early twentieth centuries. They lacked marketable personas and a supply of commodities with which to memorialize them.

As though filled with the Holy Spirit, but adapting to the nineteenth-century disciples' speaking in tongues, Sojourner Truth employed photographs as a means to communicate without writing. *Cartes de visite* might seem to circumvent the whole system of learned culture and racial stereotype that is embedded in language, so as to allow her to reach others directly. Her images, apparently unmediated, seemed to be truthful replications that communicated the essence of her real self. In photographs that she arranged and paid for, Sojourner Truth embodied herself for herself, but not in words, which would have been more convenient for her biographer. As in the 1840s, when demand for slave narratives made her own venture into that product line profitable, Truth seized upon new technology to do her work of self-representation.

As a woman whose person had been the property of others and who remembered being despised and abused, Truth may well have cherished her portraits as her own literal embodiment: as a refutation of her having deserved the abuse that she had received, as a rendering visible of the spirit otherwise trapped within. Images like hers were largely missing from American culture, even from the feminist and antislavery subcultures. Through her images, created by modern means, Truth earned money, ensured her physical survival, and, more, inserted herself into historical memory.[55] Sojourner Truth sold the shadow to support the substance when the substance was her own bodily subsistence and when the substance was her place in history. She appropriated the power of the American gaze and used it in her own mimesis.

Notes

1. Isabella's name, like the names of many African Americans, changed over the course of her lifetime. Her father was known as James Bornefree, but as a slave, Isabella was known only by her first name. Her last employers in Ulster County, New York, were named Van Wagenen, the name she used until 1843; biographers have generally used that name. However, reports in New York City and records of the Northampton Association of Education and Industry indicate that in the mid-1840s, she was known there as "Isabel or Isabella Vanwagner," "Isabel or Isabella Vanwagnen," as well as "Sojourner" and "Mrs. Sojourner." See vol. 5, Accounts, pp. 245, 251, Northampton Association of Education and Industry Records, 1836–1853 (American Antiquarian Society, Worcester, Mass.); vol. 7, Day Book No. 4, pp. 24, 246, 149, 183, 209, 210; ibid., Acts 2:1–18.
2. [Olive Gilbert and Frances Titus], *Narrative of Sojourner Truth; A Bondswoman of Olden Times, Emancipated by the New York Legislature in the Early Part of the Present Century; With a History of Her Labors and Correspondence Drawn from Her "Book of Life"* (1878; Salem, N.H., 1990), 62–71.
3. The association of photography with power comes from Susan Sontag, *On Photography* (New York, 1977), 4, 9.
4. See Karen Halttunen, *Confidence Men and Painted Women: A Study of Middle-Class Culture in America, 1830–1870* (New Haven, 1982); and John F. Kasson, *Rudeness and Civility: Manners in Nineteenth-Century Urban America* (New York, 1990).
5. *New York Journal of Commerce*, Sept. 26, 1834; *New York Commercial Advertiser*, Sept. 26, 1834; *New York Courier and Enquirer*,

Oct. 2, 1834, April 17, 1835. For a full-length treatment of Matthias, see Paul E. Johnson and Sean Wilentz, *The Kingdom of Matthias* (New York, 1994).

6. G[ilbert] Vale, *Fanaticism; Its Source and Influence, Illustrated by the Simple Narrative of Isabella in the Case of Matthias, Mr. and Mrs. B. Folger, Mr. Pierson, Mr. Mills, Catherine, Isabella, &c. &c. A Reply to W. I. Stone, with Descriptive Portraits of All the Parties, While at Sing-Sing and at Third Street.—Containing the Whole Truth—and Nothing But the Truth* (New York, 1835), pt. I, 3–6, 63.

7. On beatings, see [Gilbert and Titus], *Narrative of Sojourner Truth*, 26–27, 33. On sexual abuse, see ibid., 29–31, 81–82. The use of corporal punishment to discipline slaves has been widely acknowledged. On the sale of Truth's son, following a practice that was illegal but nonetheless common, see ibid., 44–54. Although his mother had the law on her side, she was rare among the poor and uneducated in being able to exercise her legal rights. For the most famous case of a New Yorker kidnapped and sold South, see Solomon Northup, *Twelve Years a Slave*, ed. Sue Eakin and Joseph Logsdon (Baton Rouge, 1968). The slander case grew out of the breakup of the Matthias Kingdom. Benjamin and Ann Folger accused Isabella of having attempted to poison them; she countersued and won a $125 settlement. See Vale, *Fanaticism*, pt. II, 3, 116; and Johnson and Wilentz, *Kingdom of Matthias*, 167–68.

8. Nell Irvin Painter, *Sojourner Truth: A Life, A Symbol* (New York, 1995).

9. See Jean Fagan Yellin, *Women and Sisters: The Antislavery Feminists in American Culture* (New Haven, 1989), 77–87; and Leo Braudy, *The Frenzy of Renown: Fame and Its History* (New York, 1986), 450–583.

10. See Nell Irvin Painter, "Sojourner Truth in Life and Memory: Writing the Biography of an American Exotic," *Gender and History*, 2 (Spring 1990), 3–16.

11. Isabella married Thomas, a fellow slave of John J. Dumont, in about 1814. Her *Narrative* provides a few clues as to the nature of their relationship, though it indicates that Isabella left Thomas as soon as she was free. Between about 1815 and about 1826, Isabella had five children, the names and birth dates of only four

of whom are known: Diana, born c. 1815; Peter, c. 1821; Elizabeth, c. 1825; and Sophia, c. 1826. These dates are from the Berenice Bryant Lowe Collection (Bentley Historical Library, University of Michigan, Ann Arbor).

12. Edgar J. McManus, *A History of Negro Slavery in New York* (Syracuse, 1966), 70, 173.

13. See Carleton Mabee, *Sojourner Truth: Slave, Prophet, Legend* (New York, 1993), 60–66, 217–18; and Carleton Mabee, "Sojourner Truth, Bold Prophet: Why Did She Never Learn to Read," *New York History*, 69 (Jan. 1988), 55–77. Mabee's approach to Truth epistemology is very different from mine, in that he sees literacy as the single conduit to knowledge. His definition of truth is more rigid, for he does not discuss issues of representation.

14. Frederick Douglass, "What I Found at the Northampton Association," in *History of Florence, Massachusetts. Including a Complete Account of the Northampton Association of Education and Industry*, ed. Charles A. Sheffeld (Florence, 1895), 131–32. Douglass's first wife, Anna, like Truth, did not read or write. Their children, however, were all carefully educated, the daughter in the arts, the sons in the printing trade. See William S. McFeely, *Frederick Douglass* (New York, 1991), 92, 154, 160–61, 239, 248–49, 258.

15. Vale, *Fanaticism*, pt. II, 126, pt. I, 61–63; E[lizabeth] A. Lukins, "George Thompson in Rochester," *Salem* [Ohio] *Anti-Slavery Bugle*, May 17, 1851.

16. Carl Van Wagenen, memoir and genealogy, March 8, 1991, quoting a letter of Jan. 29, 1884, found in the home of Beatrice Jordan of St. Remy, N.Y. (in Nell Irvin Painter's possession).

17. Walter J. Ong, *Orality and Literacy: The Technologizing of the Word* (London, 1982), 78–116; Plato, *Phaedrus and the Seventh and Eighth Letters*, trans. Walter Hamilton (London, 1973), 96–99. A study of nineteenth-century Black Canadians finds that literacy was often of more symbolic than material use, for it brought little advantage or disadvantage in everyday life to people so subject to racial prejudice. See Harvey Graff, *The Literacy Myth: Literacy and Social Structure in the Nineteenth-Century City* (New York, 1979), 51–91.

18. Richard D. Brown, *Knowledge Is Power: The Diffusion of Information in Early America, 1700–1865* (New York, 1989), 125–35, 184–85, 244, 283; [Gilbert and Titus], *Narrative of Sojourner Truth*, 108.

19. Gayatri Chakravorty Spivak, "Once Again into the Postcolonial Banal," paper presented at the Davis Center for Historical Studies, Princeton University, March 1, 1991 (in Painter's possession). Spivak uses the concept of overstated differences in several essays, including Gayatri Chakravorty Spivak, "Three Women's Texts and a Critique of Imperialism," in *"Race," Writing, and Difference*, ed. Henry Louis Gates, Jr. (Chicago, 1986), 262–80, and in Gayatri Chakravorty Spivak, *In Other Worlds: Essays in Cultural Politics* (New York, 1988); [Gilbert and Titus], *Narrative of Sojourner Truth*, 24.

20. Leo Braudy points out that the meaning of any performer is what her audiences want her to mean, for "to be talked about is to be part of a story, and to be part of a story is to be at the mercy of storytellers—the media and their audience." Braudy, *Frenzy of Renown*, 583, 592.

21. C. Peter Ripley to Nell Irvin Painter, Oct. 8, 1992 (in Painter's possession). C. Peter Ripley, ed., *The Black Abolitionist Papers* (5 vols., Chapel Hill, 1985–1992), IV, 81–83.

22. Virginia Woolf, *A Room of One's Own* (1929; San Diego, 1981), 26.

23. [Gilbert and Titus], *Narrative of Sojourner Truth*, xii.

24. Vol. 3, p. 229; vol. 7, pp. 304–27, Northampton Association of Education and Industry Records.

25. *International Genealogical Index* (microfiche, 9,231 fiche, Salt Lake City, 1988); [Gilbert and Titus], *Narrative of Sojourner Truth*, 276–78. Olive Gilbert may well have been associated with her Connecticut neighbor, Prudence Crandall, who lived in a nearby town and was prosecuted in 1833–1834 for her willingness to educate Black as well as White girls. George Benson, a founder of the Northampton Association, was proud of his part in Crandall's defense.

26. William L. Andrews, *To Tell a Free Story: The First Century of Afro American Autobiography, 1760–1865* (Urbana, 1986), 97, 138.

27. Printers' file (American Antiquarian Society).

28. Victoria Ortiz, *Sojourner Truth: A Self Made Woman* (Philadelphia, 1974), 92. Ortiz says that Truth's *Narrative* went through six editions, but seven appear in *The National Union Catalog, Pre 1956 Imprints* (754 vols.; London, 1968–), CX–CIX, 469.

29. Andrews, *To Tell a Free Story*, 108.

30. See, for example, Jean Baudrillard, *Le système des objects: Les essais CXXXVII* (The object system) (Paris, 1968), 14–16, 116–21; Claude Lévi-Strauss, *Conversations with Claude Lévi-Strauss*, ed. G. Charbonnier, trans. John Weightman and Doreen Weightman (London, 1969); and Nell Irvin Painter, "Difference, Slavery, and Memory: Sojourner Truth in Feminist Abolitionism," in *The Abolitionist Sisterhood: Women's Political Culture in Antebellum America*, ed. Jean Fagan Yellin and John C. Van Horne (Ithaca, 1994), 140–59.

31. This situation will presently change. Truth's 1878 *Narrative* is currently available in paperback through Oxford University Press: [Olive Gilbert], *Narrative of Sojourner Truth, A Bondswoman of Olden Time: With a History of Her Labors & Correspondence Drawn from Her "Book of Life"* (New York, 1991). A new Vintage edition of the original, 128-page, 1850 work has appeared: Margaret Washington, ed., *The Narrative of Sojourner Truth* (New York, 1993). I will republish the whole 1884 edition with a full introduction in 1995.

32. For a discussion of "puffing," often a more commercial transaction than today's "blurbing," which is not done for money, see Kelley, *Private Woman, Public Stage*, 9. Stowe's puff became the introduction to the late 1853 edition of *The Narrative of Sojourner Truth*. The original, in Stowe's hand, is in the possession of Lisa Baskin of Leeds, Massachusetts, and is used here with permission.

33. Susan Coultrap-McQuin, *Doing Literary Business: American Women Writers in the Nineteenth Century* (Chapel Hill, 1990), 86–90, 94–99.

34. Ibid., 97–98; Harriet Beecher Stowe, "Sojourner Truth, the Libyan Sibyl," *Atlantic Monthly*, 11 (April 1863), 473–81. On Stowe's "Libyan Sibyl," see Painter, "Sojourner Truth in Life and Memory"; and Patricia Hill, "Writing Out the War: Harriet

Beecher Stowe's Averted Gaze," in *Divided Houses: Gender and the Civil War*, ed. Catherine Clinton and Nina Silber (New York, 1992), 260–78.

35. I am indebted to Stowe's most recent scholarly biographer, Joan Hedrick, for this information. Joan Hedrick to Painter, Sept. 30, 1989 (in Painter's possession). See Joan Hedrick, *Harriet Beecher Stowe: A Life* (New York, 1994).

36. Stowe, "Sojourner Truth, the Libyan Sibyl," 476–77, 480. My analysis differs from that of Margaret Washington, who says that "the immediate impression of Sojourner that [Stowe] advanced was candid and memorable." Margaret Washington, "Introduction: The Enduring Legacy of Sojourner Truth," in *Narrative of Sojourner Truth*, ed. Washington, xi.

37. See *Philadelphia Woman's Advocate*, Feb. 26, 1856; Frances Dana Gage to Susan B. Anthony, [c. 1856], Papers of Frances Dana Barker Gage, 1808–1884 (Schlesinger Library, Radcliffe College, Cambridge, Mass.).

38. *Pittsburgh Saturday Visiter*, Oct. 18, 1851.

39. Frances Dana Gage, "Sojourner Truth," *Independent*, April 23, 1863.

40. Ibid.; Olive Gilbert to Sojourner Truth, Jan. 17, 1870 [c. 1870], in [Gilbert and Titus], *Narrative of Sojourner Truth*, 276–78.

41. The "Frederick, is God dead?" anecdote appears in Harriet Beecher Stowe, "The President's Message," *Independent*, Dec. 20, 1860. On it, see Mabee, *Sojourner Truth*, 83–84.

42. Elizabeth Cady Stanton, Susan B. Anthony, and Matilda Joslyn Gage, *History of Woman Suffrage* (3 vols. New York, 1881–1886), 1, 110–13.

43. Matilda Joslyn Gage (no relation to Frances Dana Gage) aided Elizabeth Cady Stanton and Susan B. Anthony in preparing the *History of Woman Suffrage*. Three later volumes, edited by Ida Husted Harper, took the story up to the passage of the Nineteenth Amendment giving women the vote nationwide. *Boston Woman's Journal*, Aug. 30, 1879; Elizabeth Griffith, *In Her Own Right: The Life of Elizabeth Cady Stanton* (New York, 1984), 176–83; Ellen Carol DuBois, "Making Women's History: Activist Historians of Women's Rights, 1880–1940," *Radical History Review*, 49 (Winter 1991), 61–84.

44. *Boston Woman's Journal*, Dec. 1, 1883, Nov. 15, Dec. 27, 1884.

45. Folder 1, Lide Parker (Smith) Meriwether Papers (Schlesinger Library).

46. "Letter from Sojourner Truth:" *Boston Commonwealth*, July 3, 1863.

47. Kathleen Collins, "Shadow and Substance: Sojourner Truth," *History of Photography*, 7 (July–Sept. 1983). 183–205, esp. 199; William C. Darrah, *Cartes de Visite in Nineteenth Century Photography* (Gettysburg, 1981), 19. The *carte de visite* appeared in the United States in the 1860s and quickly gained enormous popularity.

48. See Kathleen Collins, "The Scourged Back," *History of Photography*, 9 (Jan.–March 1985), 43–45; Kathleen Collins, "Portraits of Slave Children," ibid. (July–Sept. 1985), 187–210; and Kathleen Collins, "Photographic Fund-raising: Civil War Philanthropy," ibid., II (July–Sept. 1987), 173–87.

49. The drawing is by Charles C. Burleigh, Jr., who was a child in the late 1840s, after the breakup of the Northampton Association of Education and Industry, when Sojourner Truth still lived in Northampton. He probably drew from memory and imagination, inspired by Stowe's "Sojourner Truth, the Libyan Sibyl," Charles C. Burleigh, Jr., *Sojourner Truth* [1860s], drawing (Historic Northampton, Northampton, Mass.).

50. Stowe, "Sojourner Truth, the Libyan Sibyl," 473.

51. Susan Sontag speaks of the three-quarters gaze as conveying an "ennobling abstract relation to the future." Sontag, *On Photography*, 38.

52. On captions and viewers, see Victory Burgin, "Looking at Photographs," in *Thinking Photography*, ed. Victor Burgin (Houdmills, 1982), 144–46. The Historical Society of Battle Creek, Michigan, sells Sojourner Truth postcards to raise funds. These photographs retain the original caption, but below "SOJOURNER TRUTH" they add "Historical Society of Battle Creek, Michigan."

53. André Rouille and Bernard Marbot, *Le corps et son image: Photographies du dix neuvième siècle* (The body and its image: Photographs from the nineteenth century) (LaRochelle, 1986), 13–19, 30; Trachtenberg, *Reading American Photographs*, 28, 40; Miles Orvell, *The Real Thing: Imitation and Authenticity in*

American Culture, 1880–1940 (Chapel Hill, 1989), 77–78, 88–89; Snyder, "Inventing Photography," 21–22; John X. Berger and Oliver Richon, eds., *Other than Itself: Writing Photography* (Manchester, 1989), n.p.

54. Françoise Heilbrun, *L'invention d'un regard (1839–1918)* (The invention of a gaze, 1839–1918) (Paris, 1989), 16. For the quoted phrase, see Roland Barthes, "Rhetoric of the Image," in *Classic Essays on Photography,* ed. Alan Trachtenberg (New Haven, 1980), 269. Sigfried Kracauer adds that photographs are "surrounded with a fringe of indistinct multiple meanings." See Sigfried Kracauer, "Photography," ibid., 265.

55. Truth's attempt to embody herself through her photographs has not prevented critics from writing about her as though her existential and historic dimensions and her physical body were attenuated. Denise Riley uses Truth to interrogate the category "women," suggesting playfully that Truth might now ask, "Ain't I a fluctuating identity?" See Denise Riley, *"Am I That Name?" Feminism and the Category of 'Women' in History* (Minneapolis, 1988), 1. Donna Haraway reads Truth as a trickster figure, "a shape changer." See Donna Haraway, "Ecce Homo, Ain't (Ar'n't) I a Woman, and Inappropriate/d Others: The Human in a Post-Humanist Landscape," in *Feminists Theorize the Political,* ed. Judith Butler and Joan W. Scott (New York, 1992), 86–100. For an analysis more kindred to my own, see Richard Powell, "Sojourner Truth and the Invention of Genteel Domesticity in Her Photographic Self-Portraiture," paper delivered at the meeting of the College Art Association, New York, January 1994 (in Painter's possession).

LEGACY/
REPEAT AFTER ME

akasha (gloria) hull

My great-grandmother
compacted all her grief
until it festered as a life sore
in her side
She huddled it close
changed her pus-stained rags
in secret
Nobody in the family
knew about her shame
until they smelled the cancer
which ate her breath away

My grandmother
never found her proper nourishment
They said she ate "too much cornmeal"
Pellagra, we call it today—
a deficiency disease

which killed my grandmother
little, quick woman
who never stopped moving
until she died

My mother lives out
their lives of lack and limitation
old pains, old wounds, old angers,
resentment, grief, fear, and shame
Her milk soured in the mouth
of my baby brother
Thirty-eight years later
they cut the whole breast off
Lack of self-love, love—criticism
hardening her joints
she still holds on
holds on

All this they willed to me
this freighted legacy
I want
to cast away

I say—to myself—
repeat after me:

Throw out those old clothes
        (Let the latest and hottest fashions
        take their place)

Give the leftover spoonsful to the dog
        (God will set a fresh dish
        on the table)

Do not hoard pieces of string, clean rags,
or colored ribbons
> *(Say: What I need will be at hand*
> *when I need it)*

Give up extreme gratefulness for pennies
> *(so that thanks for thousands*
> *can be made)*

Give away love
> *(then love, and then more love*
> *will fill the place)*

Let go fear
> *(Come power*
> *and possibility)*

Expel anger
> *(Welcome joy)*

Let go of children
> *(who will then embrace you happily*
> *at every turn)*

Release pain and dis-ease
> *(Spirit pushes*
> *the healing through)*

And now
I say:
repeat after me

PART III

Telling Lives as Resistance

We can learn to work and speak when we are afraid in the same way we have learned to work and speak when we are tired. For we have been socialized to respect fear more than our own needs for language and definition, and while we wait in silence for that final luxury of fearlessness, the weight of that silence will choke us.

—AUDRE LORDE

Indian Blood (1987), Robbie McCauley. *Indian Blood*, a dance drama, was performed at The Kitchen in New York City. This work, like many of McCauley's performances, draws from her family history and focuses on the conflicting emotions of pride in and intellectual rejection of her multicultural heritage, as well as the dilemma between her patriotism and political radicalism. Photographer, Vivian Selbo, © Robbie McCauley.

I AM WRITING THIS

elaine shelly

because I stand among too many
dead bodies—black women dead of AIDS, black women
*   dead*
of breast cancer, black women dead of being black women.
I am writing because I see too many of us wounded;
huddled into corners waiting for the next slap, the next
*   morsel*
of love, the next affirmation that we are only the living
*   dead.*

I am writing because it is still too easy to call us
crazy bitches—a danger to ourselves and others, mostly
*   others.*
I am writing this because we have learned to laugh at
*   ourselves too easily.*
We laugh while cameras, for the sake of entertainment,
*   show us being dumped*

into trash bins and highlight our butts and breasts
    instead of our faces.
I am writing this because this is the third day and with it
    has come the resurrection
of the skinny black model who slinks around in a leopard
    skin.

I am writing this because I will not be conveniently
    dismissed
as a cripple who must suffer because of my sins.
I am writing this because I do not hate my body.
I am writing this because I love myself and other black
    women too damn much.

POETRY IS NOT A LUXURY

audre lorde

The quality of light by which we scrutinize our lives has direct bearing upon the product which we live, and upon the changes which we hope to bring about through those lives. It is within this light that we form those ideas by which we pursue our magic and make it realized. This is poetry as illumination, for it is through poetry that we give name to those ideas which are—until the poem—nameless and formless, about to be birthed, but already felt. That distillation of experience from which true poetry springs births thought as dream births concept, as feeling births idea, as knowledge births (precedes) understanding.

As we learn to bear the intimacy of scrutiny and to flourish within it, as we learn to use the products of that scrutiny for power within our living, those fears which rule our lives and form our silences begin to lose their control over us.

For each of us as women, there is a dark place within, where hidden and growing our true spirit rises, "beautiful / and tough as chestnut / stanchions against (y)our nightmare of weakness /"[1] and of impotence.

These places of possibility within ourselves are dark because they are ancient and hidden; they have survived and grown strong through that darkness. Within these deep places, each one of us holds an incredible reserve of creativity and power, of unexamined and unrecorded emotion and feeling. The woman's place of power within each of us is neither white nor surface; it is dark, it is ancient, and it is deep.

When we view living in the European mode only as a problem to be solved, we rely solely upon our ideas to make us free, for these were what the White fathers told us were precious.

But as we come more into touch with our own ancient, non-European consciousness of living as a situation to be experienced and interacted with, we learn more and more to cherish our feelings, and to respect those hidden sources of our power from where true knowledge and, therefore, lasting action comes.

At this point in time, I believe that women carry within ourselves the possibility for fusion of these two approaches so necessary for survival, and we come closest to this combination in our poetry. I speak here of poetry as a revelatory distillation of experience, not the sterile word play that, too often, the White fathers distorted the word *poetry* to mean—in order to cover a desperate wish for imagination without insight.

For women, then, poetry is not a luxury. It is a vital necessity of our existence. It forms the quality of the light within which we predicate our hopes and dreams toward survival and change, first made into language, then into idea, then into more tangible action. Poetry is the way we help give name to the nameless so it can be thought. The farthest horizons of our hopes and fears are cobbled by our poems, carved from the rock experiences of our daily lives.

As they become known to and accepted by us, our feelings and the honest exploration of them become sanctuaries and spawning grounds for the most radical and daring of ideas. They become a safe-house for that difference so necessary to change and the conceptualization of any meaningful action. Right now, I could name at least ten ideas I would have found intolerable or incomprehensible and frightening, except as they came after dreams and poems. This is not idle fantasy, but a disciplined attention to the true meaning of "it feels right to me." We can train ourselves to respect our feelings and to transpose them into a language so they can be shared. And where that language does not yet exist, it is our poetry which helps to fashion it. Poetry is not only dream and vision; it is the skeleton architecture of our lives. It lays the foundations for a future of change, a bridge across our fears of what has never been before.

Possibility is neither forever nor instant. It is not easy to sustain belief in its efficacy. We can sometimes work long and hard to establish one beachhead of real resistance to the deaths we are expected to live, only to have that beachhead assaulted or threatened by those canards we have been socialized to fear, or by the withdrawal of those approvals that we have been warned to seek for safety. Women see ourselves diminished or softened by the falsely benign accusations of childishness, of nonuniversality, of changeability, of sensuality. And who asks the question: Am I altering your aura, your ideas, your dreams, or am I merely moving you to temporary and reactive action? And even though the latter is no mean task, it is one that must be seen within the context of a need for true alteration of the very foundations of our lives.

The White fathers told us: I think, therefore I am. The Black mother within each of us—the poet—whispers in our dreams: I feel, therefore I can be free. Poetry coins the language to express and charter this revolutionary demand, the implementation of that freedom.

However, experience has taught us that action in the now is also necessary, always. Our children cannot dream unless they live, they cannot live unless they are nourished, and who else will feed them the real food without which their dreams will be no different from ours? "If you want us to change the world someday, we at least have to live long enough to grow up!" shouts the child.

Sometimes we drug ourselves with dreams of new ideas. The head will save us. The brain alone will set us free. But there are no new ideas still waiting in the wings to save us as women, as human. There are only old and forgotten ones, new combinations, extrapolations and recognitions from within ourselves—along with the renewed courage to try them out. And we must constantly encourage ourselves and each other to attempt the heretical actions that our dreams imply, and so many of our old ideas disparage. In the forefront of our move toward change, there is only poetry to hint at possibility made real. Our poems formulate the implications of ourselves, what we feel within and dare make real (or bring action into accordance with), our fears, our hopes, our most cherished terrors.

For within living structures defined by profit, by linear power, by institutional dehumanization, our feelings were not meant to survive. Kept around as unavoidable adjuncts or pleasant pastimes, feelings were expected to kneel to thought as women were expected to kneel to men. But women have survived. As poets. And there are no new pains. We have felt them all already. We have hidden that fact in the same place where we have hidden our power. They surface in our dreams, and it is our dreams that point the way to freedom. Those dreams are made realizable through our poems that give us the strength and courage to see, to feel, to speak, and to dare.

If what we need to dream, to move our spirits most deeply and directly toward and through promise, is discounted as a luxury, then we give up the core—the fountain—of our power, our womanness; we give up the future of our worlds.

For there are no new ideas. There are only new ways of making them felt—of examining what those ideas feel like being lived on Sunday morning at 7 A.M., after brunch, during wild love, making war, giving birth, mourning our dead—while we suffer the old longings, battle the old warnings and fears of being silent and impotent and alone, while we taste new possibilities and strengths.

Note

1. From "Black Mother Woman," first published in *From a Land Where Other People Live* (Detroit: Broadside Press, 1973), and collected in *Chosen Poems: Old and New* (New York: W. W. Norton and Company, 1982), p. 53.

MY AMERICAN HERSTORY

pearl cleage

My American Herstory begins here:

BILL OF SALE

On Tuesday, March 5th, 1833, at 1:00 P.M. the following Slaves will be sold at Potters Mart, in Charleston, S.C.

Miscellaneous lots of Negroes, mostly house servants, some for field work.

Conditions: ¹/₂ cash, balance by bond, bearing interest from date of sale. Payable in one to two years to be secured by a mortgage of the Negroes, and appraised personal security. Auctioneer will pay for the papers.

A valuable Negro woman, accustomed to all kinds of house work. Is a good plain cook, and excellent dairy maid, washes and irons. She has four children, one a girl about 13 years of age, another 7, a boy about 5, and an infant 11 months old. 2 of the children will be sold with mother, the others separately, if it best suits the purchaser.

A very valuable Blacksmith, wife and daughters, the Smith is in the prime of life, and a perfect master at his trade. His wife about 27 years old, and his daughters 12 and 10 years old have been brought up as house servants, and as such are very valuable. Also for sale 2 likely young negro wenches, one of whom is 16 the other 13, both of whom have been taught and accustomed to the duties of house servants. The 16 years old wench has one eye.

A likely yellow girl about 17 or 18 years old, has been accustomed to all kinds of house and garden work. She is sold for no fault. Sound as a dollar.

House servants: The owner of a family described herein, would sell them for a good price only, they are offered for no fault whatever, but because they can be done without, and money is need. He has been offered $1,250. They consist of a man 30 to 33 years old, who has been raised in a genteel Virginia family as house servant. Carriage driver etc. in all which he excels. His wife a likely wench of 25 to 30 raised in like manner, as chamber maid, seamstress, nurse etc., their two children, girls of 12 and 4 or 5. They are bright mulattoes, of mild tractable dispositions, unassuming manners, and of genteel appearance and well worthy the notice of a gentleman of fortune needing such.

Also 14 Negro wenches ranging from 16 to 25 years of age, all sound and capable of doing a good days work in the house or field.

My American Herstory begins here. . . .

One of the things we sometimes do in America in order to make our racial history mutually bearable is to pretend those people, *way back then*, were somehow different from us. As Black people, we distance ourselves from their degradation by thinking of them as a monolithic group of sorrowful victims, doomed to work the land and bear the lash, and somehow transformed by their victimhood into something deserving of our sympathy, but still *different*. We allow ourselves to refer to them as *slaves* instead of as Great-Grandmother Anna and Great-Aunt Abbie and second cousin Pearl. *These are things we sometimes do. . . .*

White people sometimes distance themselves by asserting that their families never owned slaves or, if they did, always treated them with care, respect, and genuine affection. After the war—in Georgia, where I live, when White people say "the war," they mean the Civil War—when they had to pay wages, such as they were, these same people are quick to assure you that they considered their maids and cooks and gardeners and chauffeurs "almost part of the family." The stage and screen success of Alfred Uhry's fairy tale, *Driving Miss Daisy*, is eloquent testimony to the popular appeal of this notion.

The problem is, these racial coping mechanisms achieve the exact opposite of the desired result. Rather than allowing the nation to "put the fact of slavery behind us" (as if such a notion were possible or desirable), these elaborate denials of reality on all fronts guarantee continued confusion, anger, resentment, and misunderstanding.

Unfortunately, I have no blueprint for meeting the challenge of getting White Americans to honestly confront slavery and its legacy, but my current work as an African American theater artist is consciously aimed at addressing the problem in my own community. I am about the business of bringing into sharp focus all those faceless, nameless, nonspecific, usually asexual Black folks who are presented as our ancestors, moving stealthily through history, identified in our collective Black consciousness as much maligned beasts of burden, victims of tragic circumstance, and an isolated role model or two.

Those were not "14 Negro wenches" being offered for "a good days work in the house or field." That was me and my sister and my mother and my daughter and my nieces and the woman across the street with the new grandbaby and the lady at the post office who likes to talk about politics and my first-grade teacher whose shoes always matched her purses and who favored white blouses with lace collars and knife-pleated skirts that fell precisely to midcalf.

Those "14 Negro wenches" were women with lovers and husbands and children and dreams and disappointments and *laughter.* They were women just like me, *which changes everything* about how I see their lives and how I see my own possibilities. Thinking *in the abstract* about European men pulling up on the shores of Africa to kidnap as many people as could be transported to America, stacked like cordwood in the filthy holds of ships sent out for this purpose and no other, is different from considering what it would be like to respond to a knock on the front door while you are watching the six o'clock news with your family and find a White man with a gun standing there who informs you that all the women under twenty-five will be taken to a breeding farm in Virginia and any men between twelve and fifty will be sent wherever there is backbreaking work to be done for free.

I want to close that gap. I want to make our history more real, more alive, and, ultimately, *more useful,* by making it *personal.*

Two things helped me to recognize this phase of my work. The first was attending a Black women scholars conference at

Spelman College several years ago. After a day spent listening to papers about Ida B. Wells-Barnett and Mary Church Terrell and Fannie Lou Hamer, I was struck by how valuable and relevant were the lessons of their lives and how few of us, *their sisters*, knew anything about these women at all.

After the day's final panel had concluded, I approached Patricia Bell-Scott, teacher, scholar, editor, and founder of *SAGE: A Scholarly Journal on Black Women,* and told her how much I had been inspired by the information they had presented. I shared with her my feeling that these women's lives were a rich source of direction for contemporary Black women and urged her to figure out a way to disseminate the information to much larger groups of sisters. She smiled and shook her head, as people often do when they're getting ready to change the direction of your life, and said simply, "That's your job."

Well, okay, but what did that mean? I'm not a scholar or a historian. My only degree is in playwrighting and dramatic literature. The Black herstorical information I had gleaned over the years was heavy on African American "sheroes," plucked whole out of context and community and presented to me as neatly sanitized Black history moments. I needed a sense of where we fit into the whole story, not a list of geniuses and warrior women who achieved greatness in spite of the formidable obstacles arrayed against them.

I got that sense from Paula Giddings's wonderful book *When and Where I Enter.* I also got the idea for my first herstory play. My 1992 play *Flyin' West* grew directly out of my strong reaction to the section "When and Where I Enter" that talks about journalist, activist, and woman extraordinaire Ida B. Wells-Barnett.

After an 1892 lynching that took the lives of two of her close friends and touched off a bloody race riot in Memphis, Tennessee, Wells-Barnett wrote a series of editorials in her newspaper, *Free Speech*, urging Negroes to pack up and become part of the country's move west.

"We should save our money and leave a town which will neither protect our lives and property, nor give us a fair trial in the courts, but takes us out and murders us in cold blood," she wrote. She also suggested that "a Winchester rifle should have a place of honor in every home. When the White man knows he runs as great a risk of biting the dust every time his victim does, he will have a greater respect for Afro American life."

The response to her words was immediate and overwhelming. Hundreds of Black people—some entire congregations led by their ministers—packed up and headed west, usually to Kansas, where several Black settlements were already thriving. In her journals, Wells-Barnett wrote, "Sometimes I wish I could gather my people in my arms and fly away West."

That image of flying Black women stayed with me. The idea of wings has always appealed to me, buoyed by many Negro folks stories of Africans taken to America in bondage, who, upon reaching these shores, looked around and decided, as my friend Joe Jennings, the jazz genius, says, that "the scene here just was not happenin'" and literally flew back home to freedom. I began considering a play about Ida B. Wells-Barnett. I thought I would call it *Flyin' West*.

Now I would like to say that I was exhilarated by the increasingly insistent presence of the first herstorical character I'd ever wanted to work with, but that would be a lie. I was intimidated by the research that would be required. I felt confined by the need to be accurate to the truth of Wells-Barnett's life or risk the wrath of family members and scholars who would write me letters to point out this inaccuracy or that one that I had missed entirely or sacrificed for the sake of dramatic structure.

I worried about all of this incessantly for a couple of days, and then, suddenly, I heard the voice of a new character in my head who gave Ida B. permission to leave and started telling me *her* story. She was an old Black woman, born into bondage in Tennessee—before "the war"—who had walked to Nicodemus, Kansas, after Emancipation, claimed the acreage promised her by the Homestead Act, and made a life for herself as a free woman. Her name was Miss Leah, and the year she was calling from was 1898. The first thing she wanted to talk about was her children.

When they sold my first baby boy offa the place, I felt like I couldn't breathe for three days, she said inside my head. *After that, I could breathe a little better, but my breasts were so full of milk, they'd soak the front of my dress. Overseer kept telling me he was gonna have to see if nigger milk was really chocolate like they said it was, so I had to stay away from him 'til my milk stopped runnin'. And one day I saw James and I told him they had sold the baby, but he already knew it. He had twenty sold offa our place by that time. Never saw any of 'em.*

When he told me that, I decided he was gonna lay eyes on at least one of his babies came through me. So next time they put us together, I told him that I was gonna be sure this time he got to see his chile before Colonel Harrison sold it. But I couldn't. Not that one or the one after or the one after the ones after that. James never saw their faces. Until we got free. Then he couldn't look at 'em long enough. That was a man who loved his children. Hug 'em and kiss 'em and take 'em everywhere he go.

I think when he saw the fever take all five of them, one by one like that . . . racin' each other to heaven . . . it just broke him down. He's waited so long to have his sons and now he was losing them all again. He was like a crazy man just before he died. So I buried him next to his children and I closed the door on that little piece of

house we had and I started walkin' west. If I'd had wings, I'd a set
out flyin' west. I needed to be someplace big enough for all my sons
and all my ghost grandbabies to roam around. Big enough for me
to think about all that sweetness they had stole from me and James
and just holler about it as loud as I want to holler.

I loved her voice the first time I heard it. I especially liked
the fact that she said my working title back to me in the context of her story, since I am old enough now to recognize a sign
when I see one, and that she saw the theater as I did: *as a hol-*
lering place. Here was a way into all the facts I had absorbed
through my own imagination and a character I was creating
from scratch; but I was still a little nervous. I didn't know much
about Nicodemus, even less about the Homestead Act, and
almost nothing about life on the frontier that didn't include
John Wayne. How was I going to make it real?

I didn't need to worry. The material I wanted was abundant
and available. In addition to Sister Giddings and some books
about the Black West by William Loren Katz, I actually read
the Homestead Act before moving on to actual women's
diaries and letters home and journals of farm life. I was struck
by the similarity of our concerns and theirs—childbirth, love,
family, spirit, work, joy, regret, and always dreams of something
better, as Sophie, another character in *Flyin' West*, says, "something free and fine and all our own."

I began to understand that this play was also a place where
I could continue to explore a problem that had dominated my
writing for the past several years—domestic violence. I won-
dered how frontier women handled abuse by their husbands.
That's when Miss Leah introduced me to her extended family
and I realized that one of them was being beaten by her self-
hating mulatto husband, Frank. Add to the mixture Sophie's
belief in Ida B.'s advice about the necessity for that Winchester

rifle, Miss Leah's knowledge of some secret recipes from Africa, and a slowly blooming midlife love affair, and I knew I was ready to write.

I was relieved when I completed the script and gratified when people told me how "real" the characters were, since I didn't want to make a history pageant where you watch it because it's supposed to be good for you rather than because you care. I had enjoyed the process, learned a lot, and created a story that let me share the information without compromising artistically or politically.

Perhaps most amazing to me, the play was embraced by diverse audiences across the country who seemed to love Miss Leah as much as I did. Although the play explored issues of Black nationalism, domestic violence, African American color madness, and the nature of justice, what Black people and White people, men and women, wrote or called to tell me was how much Miss Leah reminded them of their own grandmothers. *So far, so good.*

My next play, *Blues for an Alabama Sky*, began with my love of the Harlem renaissance and my desire to create some characters who were fully a part of that time and through whose eyes we could be, too. I wanted to present the rich, complex specificity of a community of Black artists who are often gussied up and made so respectable before we get to meet them that their wild bohemianness disappears completely.

And that is a tragedy. The era has a rich cast of characters who sometimes seem more theatrical than any I could conjure up. I loved their charisma, their courage, and their absolute individuality, and I was stunned by the overlapping realities of their lives. Young Adam Clayton Powell marrying a beautiful Cotton Club star at the very moment he was assuming the leadership of his more straitlaced father's Abyssinian Baptist

Church, at the time the nation's largest Protestant congregation, Black or White.

Birth control pioneer Margaret Sanger opening a birth control clinic on 126th Street and being allowed to state her case to Powell's congregation, although Black nationalist Marcus Garvey said her work amounted to nothing more than genocide. Trainloads of small-town southern Negroes arriving in Harlem daily, looking for jobs and nightlife and freedom from the threat of White violence that had circumscribed their lives and taking up residence in crowded apartments next door to the dancers and jazz players and actors and poets who made the renaissance the shimmering moment that it was.

But I was also curious about what happened to the glittering members of the Harlem literati with the advent of the Great Depression, another period that held great interest for me. What happened when the clubs closed, when the White patrons went broke and, as Langston Hughes remembers in the first volume of his autobiography, *The Big Sea*, the Negro was no longer in vogue.

So I set the play in Harlem at the end of the renaissance, circa 1930, and I listened for the voices of the people who would introduce me to the neighborhood. I knew from my experience with *Flyin' West* that I didn't want to work with real people. I wanted to work with their imaginary friends and neighbors—the people who attended Abyssinian and sat in the pew behind the famous folks; the people who danced and gambled and drank bathtub gin at the rent parties immortalized by Hughes in poems like "The Weary Blues." I was listening for all those living souls in Harlem who made the history even though they didn't make it into the history books.

It didn't take long for them to arrive in my head, and they were a passionate and talkative bunch, too. Angel, a beautiful

Cotton Club backup singer whose Italian gangster lover has just left her for his wife. Doc, a jazz-loving obstetrician at Harlem Hospital known for shouting, "Let the good times roll!" at post-delivery celebrations and who is secretly aching to fall in love. Delia, a virginal social worker on the staff at the Sanger clinic who loves her work, and the bohemian friends who have taken her under their wings. Leland, a recent transplant from Tuskegee, Alabama, whose small-town life has not prepared him for missing "that Alabama sky where the stars are so thick it's bright as day," and Guy, a costume designer who carries a straight razor to discourage gay bashers, parties with Langston Hughes and Bruce Nugent, and is making plans to move to Paris and work with Josephine Baker because he understands that for prospects "you gotta look past 125th Street."

And, of course, they brought their problems with them. How to find a way to make a living as artists. How to fall in love. How to improve the health of the people of Harlem. How to protect yourself without sacrificing your friends. How to tell the difference between dreams and visions. How to accept people for what they are without being destroyed by what you wish they were. And then there's the question of integrity and the complexity of abortion. . . .

I consider both *Blues for an Alabama Sky* and *Flyin' West* to be propaganda in the best sense of the word. I am unabashedly attempting to lure people into looking beyond those stolid Black history moments to see the fully functional human beings behind the carefully backlit calendar portraits. I am consciously trying to make Black audiences see themselves up there talking in the light, because I believe Amiri Baraka was right when he said, "If the beautiful see themselves, they will love themselves," *and* that Che Guevara was right, too, when he said, "True revolutions are always guided by feelings of great love."

I consider the plays to be subversive, introducing us, as they both do, to characters and actions that would probably be objected to vehemently in my community in the places where intellect or religion or conformity is allowed the upper hand.

When the women in *Flyin' West* handled their abuser by feeding him a piece of poison apple pie, burying him in the prairie, and heading for the harvest dance, audience members who probably on a conscious level consider murder an unacceptable response to wife-beating *cheered.* A few even lingered after the show to ask me if I really had a recipe for that pie, *but that's not this story.*

When Guy, the designer in *Blues,* confronts Leland's anti-gay sentiments in no uncertain terms and an invitation to step outside, straight Black men in the audience who I know to be homophobic in their daily lives nodded their brotherly support and approval.

They also absorbed a little real history when Sophie talks of coming west in a group organized by the legendarily charismatic Pap Singleton, who once claimed, "I am the whole cause of the Kansas migration." Or when Miss Leah mourned ten children sold away before Emancipation. Or when Guy describes the Harlem drag balls where hundreds of unapologetically gay Black men danced in floor-length gowns or white tie and tails, depending upon their preference. Or when Delia bemoans the bombing of a birth control clinic and Angel confronts the reality of homeless people sleeping on the streets outside her window.

And if I do it right, it's not the kind of history that puts you to sleep or sets such an impossibly high standard of correct behavior that only a living saint could be expected to come close to achieving it in this lifetime. I'm trying to write the kind of herstory that lets us see ourselves, *up there in the light,* falling in love and changing the world and having our babies and walking to Kansas and going to nightclubs with our friends and groping for the truth and drinking champagne in Josephine's dressing room at the Folies-Bergère—and did I say changing the world and falling in love and acting a fool and rising to the occasion *because we can, and we did, and we do, and we better* because the time is getting very late and, as Sister Robbie McCauley says, "History will go down like history will go down," and if I don't tell the story straight, *then who will?*

My friend Alice Walker says, "Resistance is the secret of joy," which is why I love my work. My friend Toni Cade Bambara said, *"The responsibility of an artist representing an oppressed people is to make revolution irresistible,"* which is why I take it all seriously. But I don't forget to let Bessie Smith or Fats Waller sit in every now and then.

"I HAD TO TELL THE TRUTH"

Testimony to the U.S. Senate Judiciary Committee's
Confirmation Hearings for Judge Clarence Thomas

anita f. hill

Ms. Hill: Mr. Chairman, Senator Thurmond, members of the committee, my name is Anita F. Hill, and I am a Professor of Law at the University of Oklahoma.

I was born on a farm in Okmulgee County, Oklahoma, in 1956. I am the youngest of thirteen children. I had my early education in Okmulgee County. My father, Albert Hill, is a farmer in that area. My mother's name is Erma Hill. She is also a farmer and a housewife.

My childhood was one of a lot of hard work and not much money, but it was one of solid family affection as represented by my parents. I was reared in a religious atmosphere in the Baptist faith, and I have been a member of the Antioch Baptist Church in Tulsa, Oklahoma, since 1983. It is a very warm part of my life at the present time.

For my undergraduate work, I went to Oklahoma State University, and graduated from there in 1977. I am attaching to the statement a copy of my résumé for further details of my education.

THE CHAIRMAN: It will be included in the record.

MS. HILL: Thank you.

I graduated from the university with academic honors and proceeded to the Yale Law School, where I received my J.D. degree in 1980.

Upon graduation from law school, I became a practicing lawyer with the Washington, D.C., firm of Wald, Harkrader & Ross. In 1981, I was introduced to now-Judge Thomas by a mutual friend. Judge Thomas told me that he was anticipating a political appointment and asked if I would be interested in working with him. He was, in fact, appointed as Assistant Secretary of Education for Civil Rights. After he had taken that post, he asked if I would become his assistant, and I accepted that position.

In my early period there, I had two major projects. First was an article I wrote for Judge Thomas's signature on the education of minority students. The second was the organization of a seminar on high-risk students, which was abandoned, because Judge Thomas transferred to the EEOC, where he became the chairman of that office.

During this period at the Department of Education, my working relationship with Judge Thomas was positive. I had a good deal of responsibility and independence. I thought he respected my work and that he trusted my judgment.

After approximately three months of working there, he asked me to go out socially with him. What happened next and telling the world about it are the two most difficult things, experiences of my life. It is only after a great deal of agonizing consideration and a number of sleepless nights that I am able to talk of these unpleasant matters to anyone but my close friends.

I declined the invitation to go out socially with him, and explained to him that I thought it would jeopardize what at the time I considered to be a very good working relationship. I had a normal social life with other men outside of the office. I believed then, as now, that having a social relationship with a person who was supervising my work would be ill advised. I was very uncomfortable with the idea and told him so.

I thought that by saying "no" and explaining my reasons, my employer would abandon his social suggestions. However, to my regret, in the following few weeks he continued to ask me out on several occasions. He pressed me to justify my reasons for saying "no" to him. These incidents took place in his office or mine. They were in the form of private conversations which would not have been overheard by anyone else.

My working relationship became even more strained when Judge Thomas began to use work situations to discuss sex. On these occasions, he would call me into his office for reports on education issues and projects or he might suggest that because of the time pressures of his schedule, we go to lunch to a government cafeteria. After a brief discussion of work, he would turn the conversation to a discussion of sexual matters. His conversations were very vivid.

He spoke about acts that he had seen in pornographic films involving such matters as women having sex with animals, and films showing group sex or rape scenes. He talked about pornographic materials depicting individuals with large penises, or large breasts involved in various sex acts.

On several occasions Thomas told me graphically of his own sexual prowess. Because I was extremely uncomfortable talking about sex with him at all, and particularly in such a graphic way, I told him that I did not want to talk about these subjects. I would also try to change the subject to education matters or to nonsexual personal matters, such as his background or his beliefs. My efforts to change the subject were rarely successful.

Throughout the period of these conversations, he also from time to time asked me for social engagements. My reactions to these conversations was to avoid them by limiting opportunities for us to engage in extended conversations. This was difficult because at the time, I was his only assistant at the Office of Education or Office for Civil Rights.

During the latter part of my time at the Department of Education, the social pressures and any conversation of his offensive behavior ended. I began both to believe and hope that our working relationship could be a proper, cordial, and professional one.

When Judge Thomas was made Chair of the EEOC, I needed to face the question of whether to go with him. I was asked to do so and I did. The work itself was interesting, and at that time, it appeared that the sexual overtures, which had so troubled me, had ended.

I also faced the realistic fact that I had no alternative job. While I might have gone back to private practice, perhaps in my old firm, or at another, I was dedicated to civil rights work and my first choice was to be in that field. Moreover, at that time the Department of Education, itself, was a dubious venture. President Reagan was seeking to abolish the entire department.

For my first months at the EEOC, where I continued to be an assistant to Judge Thomas, there were no sexual conversations or overtures. However, during the fall and winter of 1982, these began again. The comments were random, and ranged from pressing me about why I didn't go out with him, to remarks about my personal appearance. I remember him saying that someday I would have to tell him the real reason that I wouldn't go out with him.

He began to show displeasure in his tone and voice and his demeanor in his continued pressure for an explanation. He commented on what I was wearing in terms of whether it made me more or less sexually attractive. The incidents occurred in his inner office at the EEOC.

One of the oddest episodes I remember was an occasion in which Thomas was drinking a Coke in his office. He got up from the table, at which we were working, went over to his desk to get the Coke, looked at the can and asked, "Who has put pubic hair on my Coke?"

On other occasions he referred to the size of his own penis as being larger than normal and he also spoke on some occasions of the pleasures he had given to women with oral sex. At this point, late 1982, I began to feel severe stress on the job. I began to be concerned that Clarence Thomas might take out his anger with me by degrading me or not giving me important assignments. I also thought that he might find an excuse for dismissing me.

In January 1983, I began looking for another job. I was handicapped because I feared that if he found out he might make it difficult for me to find other employment, and I might be dismissed from the job I had.

Another factor that made my search more difficult was that this was during a period of a hiring freeze in the government. In February 1983, I was hospitalized for five days on an emergency basis for acute stomach pain which I attributed to stress on the job. Once out of the hospital, I became more committed to find other employment and sought further to minimize my contact with Thomas.

This became easier when Allyson Duncan became office director because most of my work was then funneled through her and I had contact with Clarence Thomas mostly in staff meetings.

In the spring of 1983, an opportunity to teach at Oral Roberts University opened up. I participated in a seminar, taught an afternoon session in a seminar at Oral Roberts University. The dean of the university saw me teaching and inquired as to whether I would be interested in pursuing a career in teaching, beginning at Oral Roberts University. I agreed to take the job, in large part because of my desire to escape the pressures I felt at the EEOC due to Judge Thomas.

When I informed him that I was leaving in July, I recall that his response was that now I would no longer have an excuse for not going out with him. I told him that I still preferred not to do so. At some time after that meeting, he asked if he could take me to dinner at the end of the term. When I declined, he assured me that the dinner was a professional courtesy only and not a social invitation. I reluctantly agreed to accept that invitation but only if it was at the very end of a working day.

On, as I recall, the last day of my employment at the EEOC in the summer of 1983, I did have dinner with Clarence Thomas. We went directly from work to a restaurant near the office. We talked about the work that I had done both at Education and at the EEOC. He told me that he was pleased with all of it except for an article and speech that I had done for him while we were at the Office for Civil Rights. Finally he made a comment that I will vividly remember. He said, that if I ever told anyone of his behavior that it would ruin his career. This was not an apology, nor was it an explanation. That was his last remark about the possibility of our going out, or reference to his behavior.

In July 1983, I left the Washington, D.C., area and have had minimal contacts with Judge Clarence Thomas since. I am, of course, aware from the press that some questions have been raised about conversations I had with Judge Clarence Thomas after I left the EEOC.

From 1983 until today I have seen Judge Thomas only twice. On one occasion I needed to get a reference from him and on another, he made a public appearance at Tulsa. On one occasion he called me at home and we had an inconsequential conversation. On one occasion he called me without reaching me and I returned the call without reaching him and nothing came of it. I have, at least on three occasions, been asked to act as a conduit to him for others.

I knew his secretary, Diane Holt. We had worked together both at EEOC and Education. There were occasions on which I spoke to her and on some of these occasions, undoubtedly, I passed on some casual comment to then-Chairman Thomas. There were a series of calls in the first three months of 1985, occasioned by a group in Tulsa which wished to have a civil rights conference. They wanted Judge Thomas to be the speaker and enlisted my assistance for this purpose.

I did call in January and February to no effect and finally suggested to the person directly involved, Susan Cahall, that she put the matter into her own hands and call directly. She did so in March 1985.

In connection with that March invitation, Ms. Cahall wanted conference materials for the seminar, and some research was needed. I was asked to try and get the information and did attempt to do so. There was another call about another possible conference in July 1985.

In August 1987, I was in Washington, D.C., and I did call Diane Holt. In the course of this conversation she asked me how long I was going to be in town and I told her. It is recorded in the messages as August 15, it was in fact August 20. She told me about Judge Thomas's marriage and I did say, congratulations.

It is only after a great deal of agonizing consideration that I am able to talk of these unpleasant matters to anyone, except my closest friends as I have said before. These last few days have been very trying and very hard for me, and it hasn't just been the last few days this week. It has actually been over a month now that I have been under the strain of this issue. Telling the world is the most difficult experience of my life, but it is very close to hav[ing] to live through the experience that occasioned this meeting. I may have used poor judgment early on in my relationship with this issue. I was aware, however, that telling at any point in my career could adversely affect my future career. And I did not want, early on, to burn all the bridges to the EEOC.

As I said, I may have used poor judgment. Perhaps I should have taken angry or even militant steps, both when I was in the agency or after I had left it, but I must confess to the world that the course that I took seemed the better, as well as the easier approach.

I declined any comment to newspapers, but later when Senate staff asked me about these matters, I felt that I had a duty to report. I have no personal vendetta against Clarence Thomas. I seek only to provide the committee with information which it may regard as relevant.

It would have been more comfortable to remain silent. I took no initiative to inform anyone. But when I was asked by a representative of this committee to report my experience, I felt that I had to tell the truth. I could not keep silent.

BARBARA SMITH

A Home Girl with a Mission

patricia bell-scott

INTRODUCTION

Writer-activist Barbara Smith was born in 1946 and reared with her twin sister, Beverly, by a grandmother and aunt after the death of their mother. From womanfolk Barbara inherited a love of African American cultural traditions, as well as a commitment to social change. This commitment is reflected in her politics and a lifetime of advocacy on behalf of people of color and women's and lesbian/gay issues.

Although known primarily for her activism, Barbara is first of all a writer. She has written numerous essays, poems, and short stories. She is also editor of several major works—including All the Women Are White, All the Blacks Are Men, But Some of Us Are Brave: Black Women's Studies *(with Akasha Hull and Patricia Bell-Scott),* Home Girls: A Black Feminist Anthology, *and* The Reader's Companion to U.S. Women's History *(with Wilma Mankiller, Gwendolyn Mink, Marysa Navarro, and Gloria*

Steinem)—and is cofounder of Kitchen Table: Women of Color Press. Her current project is the first history of African American lesbians and gays in the United States.

In this conversation, she describes the origins, rewards, and consequences of an activist life, as well as the marginalization of African American lesbians and gays by conventional Black, women, and lesbian and gay organizations. She also reflects on her personal journey toward self-acceptance.

LETTERS FROM HOME

There has been a tragic occurrence! I've lost my favorite watermelon pin. It was enamel, beautifully done in red and glazed like pottery. Small, very nice, no more than an inch. And it looked just like a slice of watermelon. You know, I could tell a lot about people by how they reacted to my watermelon pin. Those who were obviously down with me would laugh and say, "Oh, that's so wonderful." Then there were other people who couldn't laugh and they'd ask, "What is *that* for? What does it represent?" So I'd think of little answers like I belong to an organization where we eat watermelon once every month, even when it's out of season. Occasionally some Black person would say, "Well, don't you think that's racist?" I'd say, "No, it's not racist; watermelon is a fruit! Now, if I had a White person up here on my lapel, *then* we could say that that was an embodiment or a depiction of someone or something that could be potentially racist."

I have many watermelon things in my home. To me, they are the perfect food. Many of my friends know that I love them, so I am constantly acquiring representations. When I went to visit the Black woman filmmaker Michelle Parkerson and she too had a house full of watermelons, I thought, Great minds run together. I also have an article by Vertamae Grosvenor titled "A Watermelon Fan Comes Out of the Closet," which I send to people on occasion. In this piece, Vertamae writes about her love of watermelons as an evocation of Black culture. I also see them as a symbol of Black culture generally and perhaps even Black female culture. My aunt who raised me and my sister in Cleveland, Ohio, told us that they called watermelons letters from home. They were precious.

FAMILY LEGACIES

The people I was raised by worked really, really hard, mostly as domestics. We were one of those respectable Black families, where people did what they were supposed to do—went to work, took care of their children, stayed clear of illegal activities, and refrained from becoming a public nuisance. We were the kind of ordinary Black family that many White folks do not believe existed. And we were like everyone else we knew.

Even though there wasn't a huge amount open to them, people in our family valued education highly. A couple of great-aunts, my grandmother's sisters, went to Spelman in the early 1900s. Once while I was looking through the college archives, I found a penny postcard from my aunt Rosa, whom I grew up with. She had taken normal school courses there. Another great-aunt who died before I was born spoke on the emancipation of Turkish women at her graduation from the Spelman high school division. Now that explains to me in part why I'm such a staunch feminist. I come by it honestly from family.

My twin sister, Beverly, and I were raised by our grandmother and aunts. Our mother, who was a single parent and worked outside the home, died in 1956, when we were only nine. Our grandmother was like the Black women generals Alice Walker describes in some of her writings. Rules were strictly enforced, and there was none of this positive reinforcement so popular today. There was no raving or pay for grades. Are you kidding? When we brought home straight-A report cards, our family would say, "That's nice." Excellence was simply expected. At this point in my life, I think that I have put my grandmother's ways into perspective and have come to appreciate many of the things she taught me. Besides usable skills like sewing, she taught me self-discipline, which is very important. There was never any sense of day-to-day uncertainty in our lives. Whatever grown people said, whatever the plan was, whatever was supposed to happen, happened.

My mother, Hilda, was the youngest of my grandmother's three children and the only one to finish college. She tried to get certified to teach in the Cleveland public school system, but because the conditions in the ghetto schools were so demoralizing, she returned to her job as head cashier at a local supermarket. Before that, she had been a nurse's aide. I will never forget telling a White woman therapist about my mother being a college graduate and the kinds of jobs she had and having this therapist tell me that my mother obviously had a self-image problem. The diagnosis was that I had a similar problem—no self-confidence. What this White woman did not understand was that there had been generations of Black college-educated people, men and women, who were denied jobs that their education had prepared them for. And maybe my mother did have a self-image problem—after all, she was a Black single mother in the 1940s with two little children and she had to take any damn job she could find! In her day, there were Black folks with Ph.D.s working in the U.S. postal service because they couldn't get jobs elsewhere. That's just the way that was.

A NATURAL CALLING

I'm kind of a natural activist. It's a tendency or capacity that probably would have found an outlet eventually—but because I came of age in the civil rights era, I had a vehicle for channeling my justifiable anger at the circumstances under which I saw my community living. By the time I was eight I noticed that things were not fair—that mostly Brown people lived in tenements and only White people lived in mansions. I also had an endless list of questions like: Why were there Black people and why were there White people? Why didn't any White people live in our neighborhood? Why were there only White people on television? Why were all of our teachers White but all of the children Black? Why, when a White person knocked on our door—though this almost never happened and then it was an insurance salesman or someone like that—was there anxiety in the air that my sister and I could grasp? Why was the tension so strong when my aunt went to a department store to buy stockings? And why did the clerks ignore her? I wanted to know why about all of this.

The first demonstration I ever went to was in the early 1960s, when I was in high school. Bruce Klunder, a White minister, was killed protesting the building of a new elementary school that would be segregated. He lay down in a ditch in front of some construction equipment, and by accident or design, the workers rolled over him. I remember going to protest rallies after that. My sister and I also stayed home on the Monday of the school boycott, going instead to a Freedom School that had been set up in a neighborhood church. I think my family was basically supportive of our participation in these demonstrations because they were race women. They supported the NAACP, and my grandmother always worked at the polls. They also had migrated from the South, so they knew even better than I did the horrors of U.S. apartheid that the movement was working to change.

I began my activism early, and eventually I came to identify as a Black feminist, a lesbian, and a socialist. I also believe that the Combahee Collective—of which I was a cofounder and which functioned from 1974 to 1981 in Boston—was one of the most significant groups to come out of any movement. The collective had a series of retreats that brought together Black women artists and activists who were committed to feminism and political organizing. We made a conscious effort to look at how systems of oppression were connected to each other. We understood that dealing with sexual politics didn't mean that you weren't a race woman, and that speaking out about homophobia didn't mean that you didn't want to end poverty.

A lifetime of activism has had several major consequences for me. It has meant being outside of the academy, but despite my love of teaching I never really envisioned a traditional academic career. Needless to say, it has meant working hard for long hours and for little, if any, pay. It has also meant sometimes putting my writing on hold, particularly the fiction. However, I wasn't raised to think that everything was about me. Black feminism meant to me that I had a responsibility to help build and provide resources for other women of color; and a commitment to struggle requires certain sacrifices. Now I'm not saying that you have to take a vow of poverty, but I do not think that you can vacation on the Riviera every summer and still be about struggle.

There *are* tangible rewards to the activist life. I've seen a lot of change in my lifetime. When I was born into segregation in 1946, most Black people in this country could not vote; those who did or tried to vote did so on pain of death. And the women in my family could not try on a hat in a southern department store—and that included Washington, D.C. I never bend over a public water fountain without realizing that once this would have been a revolutionary act. I know these things seem small, particularly to young people who have never lived the other way. We still have a long way to go, but I know that it took revolutionary commitment to get to this point.

AN INVISIBLE SISTER

Despite all my years of activism on behalf of Black, women's, and lesbian and gay issues, there are times when I really feel like a stranger. At the twenty-fifth anniversary of Stonewall, the underrepresentation of people of color was demoralizing. It reminded me of Ralph Ellison's brilliant book *The Invisible Man*, which captures an experience that almost every person of color can identify with. Very few lesbian and gay men of color, including myself, are ever invited to the leadership summits called by White gay leaders. Being omitted from a meeting or invitation list might seem at first thought like a small thing; the larger issue is about the disenfranchisement of women and men of color within the movement.

I'm convinced that our disempowerment at this moment in history is directly related to a push to mainstream the lesbian and gay movement in the United States. Bruce Bawer's book, *A Place at the Table*, comes out of this mainstreaming effort, which is problematic for me because I really have no interest in reinforcing or dealing with the establishment. As a radical, I want to see it destroyed. I want a nonhierarchical, nonexploitative society in which profit is not the sole motivation for every single decision made by the government or individuals. And if the lesbian and gay movement's motto becomes "A place at the table" in the present system, I have to ask, what am I as a Black woman going to be doing at this table—carrying a tray? Handing someone a dish? A place at the table? Not likely. It really doesn't work for me.

Black women's organizations should be at the forefront of the fight against homophobia in the Black community. They need to indicate their support of all Black women, regardless of sexual orientation. Unfortunately, many of them are afraid to stand publicly in support of gay and lesbian issues. They fear the inevitable charge that they are just a bunch of lesbians, which has been said about all women's groups.

One painful experience that I have over and over again is when prominent Black women leaders who are closeted pull me aside at a conference or some gathering to say, "Barbara, I'm so glad you're doing what you're doing. You're doing wonderful work, girl, and you just go on and do it! Go on, sister, I'm right behind you." Yet they are not about to say on the stage or anywhere publicly, "As a lesbian I'm so proud that Barbara's a lesbian, too. She has helped me be proud as a lesbian." They're not able or willing to do that. These encounters always remind me of the title of Audre Lorde's book *Sister Outsider*. It's an oxymoron because a sister is obviously someone inside the family, close, a home girl. But the sister with the lesbian feminist politics like Audre's or mine is also an outsider.

WRITING AS EMPOWERMENT

I wanted to be a writer as soon as I found out that you could be one. James Baldwin was key in that. I was first introduced to him through *Go Tell It on the Mountain,* thanks to Aunt LaRue, who worked at the Cleveland Public Library as a clerk-typist. She would bring home shopping bags full of books, and my sister and I would devour them. When I read *Go Tell It on the Mountain,* I was thunderstruck. Here was a book that described a little guy, a main character, who was so much like me. He was shy; he liked to write; he was not happy; and he saw so many things. Until I read Baldwin I never knew that one could write about being Black and poor and get published. I assumed that the only way you could write a book or be a novelist was to write about well-off White people. I thought to myself, This is incredible writing. Maybe I could do that, too. After I read Baldwin, that was it.

Of all my writings, the essay "Toward a Black Feminist Literary Criticism" (1978) continues to hold a special place for me. I think that there are probably moments in every artist's life where you feel that you didn't necessarily create what was there but were instead the vehicle for it to be manifested. Looking back, I feel that way about this essay. It defined a moment, a feeling, a new field, and possibilities. It was a piece after which other things could be written on the topic. And it is still the subject of debate and dialogue. It also fascinates me when men and women who are not of African origin tell me what this essay has meant to them. That says something to me, not because I seek validation from people who are unlike me, but because that piece is very Black, very female, and very lesbian.

With the increased acceptance of research and writing about Black women, I sometimes reflect on the introduction to our book *All the Women Are White, All the Blacks Are Men, But Some of Us Are Brave: Black Women's Studies.* In that piece we said that the goal of Black women's studies is to save Black women's lives. We didn't say it was to get tenure, a book contract, or a certain salary. We said it was about saving lives, and we meant *every* Black woman—not just those lucky enough to get higher education and do college or university teaching or research. We meant the Black woman who's never going to read any of our damn books.

I am writing the first book on the history of African American lesbians and gays. I hope, with this project, to give us back to ourselves and to empower people. Almost all of my writing has been about empowerment and about trying to say to people of color, to women, and to lesbians and gay men that you are really worth something, you are important, you have a history to be proud of. There is no reason to be ashamed.

COMING HOME

For me, moving into midlife has had advantages. One of these is a more balanced perspective on life—or maybe even sometimes wisdom. This new perspective has given me a clear vision of what my limits and priorities are, as well as the relative unimportance of what most people think of me. The older I get and the longer I'm here, the more adjusted I become to being a human being on this planet.

I have developed an appreciation for simple acts of self-care—like a daytime nap, eating on time, and sitting quietly after a bout of running around. Self-acceptance is another thing that has come to me. I'm having the time of my life doing the work I love. I'm not saying that my life has been perfect or that I have no regrets, because there have been mistakes and disappointments. But midlife teaches that I don't have to repeat those experiences again, and that is a comforting thought. After all these years of hard work, I'm coming home to me. And the feeling is good. Really good.

IN ANSWER TO THE QUESTION

Have You Ever Considered Suicide?

kate rushin

Suicide??!!
Gurl, is you crazy?
I'm scared I'm not gonna live long enough
As it is

I'm scared to death of high places
Fast cars
Rare diseases
Muggers
Drugs
Electricity
And folks who work roots

Now what would I look like
Jumping off of something

I got everything to do
And I ain't got time for that
Let me tell you
If you ever hear me
Talking about killing my frail self
Come and get me
Sit with me until that spell passes
Cause it will
And if they ever
Find me laying up somewhere
Don't let them tell you it was suicide
Cause it wasn't

I'm scared of high places
Fast-moving trucks
Muggers
Electricity
Drugs
Folks who work roots
And home-canned string beans

Now with all I got
To worry about
What would I look like
Killing myself

PART IV

TELLING LIVES AS TRANSFORMATION

These women heal us by telling our stories,
by embodying emotion that our everydays can't hold.

—ELIZABETH ALEXANDER

She (1997), Wini "Akissi" McQueen. The *She* Quilt, completed in 1994, is a 60″ × 90″ pictorial representation of Black southern womanhood. Commissioned by the Harriet Tubman Museum in Macon, this story quilt narrates the lives of famous and everyday women of the local area from the 1800s through the present. Photographer, Nancy Bennett Evelyn, © Wini McQueen.

MOVIN' AND STEPPIN'

akasha (gloria) hull

There are times when
one needs to move—
to newer places
wider spaces

exchange the pond
        for the ocean
and jump right in
(it don't matter if your hair
gets wet or briny)

Mothers can tell you
shoes get too tight
and clothes grow old

How can you be Cinderella
        in the same tired frumpy frog gown

let alone Nerfertiti or Cleopatra
      conquering the Nile

It just won't do.

Generally speaking,
it's hard for people's eyes
      to readjust
There you stand—
      a brand new thang
and they keep talking to someone
      you left behind long time ago
      (and swear you never want to see again)

Jive action like that
can push you back—
into the Dark Ages, a closet,
some fancy trickbag or claustrophobic hole

Take a stroll
down different streets
where there are flowers that you can't name
and sights you've never seen before

Where the air breathes fresher
      and people take you for a stranger

And you can keep on walking
hightime stepping getting up walking
into that future self
you got to be

THE TRANSFORMATION OF SILENCE INTO LANGUAGE AND ACTION

audre lorde

I have come to believe over and over again that what is most important to me must be spoken, made verbal and shared, even at the risk of having it bruised or misunderstood. That the speaking profits me, beyond any other effect. I am standing here as a Black lesbian poet, and the meaning of all that waits upon the fact that I am still alive, and might not have been. Less than two months ago I was told by two doctors, one female and one male, that I would have to have breast surgery, and that there was a 60 to 80 percent chance that the tumor was malignant. Between that telling and the actual surgery, there was a three-week period of the agony of an involuntary reorganization of my entire life. The surgery was completed, and the growth was benign.

But within those three weeks, I was forced to look upon myself and my living with a harsh and urgent clarity that has left me still shaken but much stronger. This is a situation faced by many women, by some of you here today. Some of what I experienced during that time has helped elucidate for me much of what I feel concerning the transformation of silence into language and action.

In becoming forcibly and essentially aware of my mortality, and of what I wished and wanted for my life, however short it might be, priorities and omissions became strongly etched in a merciless light, and what I most regretted were my silences. Of what had I *ever* been afraid? To question or to speak as I believed could have meant pain, or death. But we all hurt in so many different ways, all the time, and pain will either change or end. Death, on the other hand, is the final silence. And that might be coming quickly, now, without regard for whether I had ever spoken what needed to be said, or had only betrayed myself into small silences, while I planned someday to speak, or waited for someone else's words. And I began to recognize a source of power within myself that comes from the knowledge that while it is most desirable not to be afraid, learning to put fear into a perspective gave me great strength.

I was going to die, if not sooner then later, whether or not I had ever spoken myself. My silences had not protected me. Your silence will not protect you. But for every real word spoken, for every attempt I had ever made to speak those truths for which I am still seeking, I had made contact with other women while we examined the words to fit a world in which we all believed, bridging our differences. And it was the concern and caring of all those women which gave me strength and enabled me to scrutinize the essentials of my living.

The women who sustained me through that period were Black and White, old and young, lesbian, bisexual, and heterosexual, and we all shared a war against the tyrannies of silence.

They all gave me a strength and concern without which I could not have survived intact. Within those weeks of acute fear came the knowledge—within the war we are all waging with the forces of death, subtle and otherwise, conscious or not—I am not only a casualty, I am also a warrior.

What are the words you do not yet have? What do you need to say? What are the tyrannies you swallow day by day and attempt to make your own, until you will sicken and die of them, still in silence? Perhaps for some of you here today, I am the face of one of your fears. Because I am woman, because I am Black, because I am lesbian, because I am myself—a Black woman warrior poet doing my work—come to ask you, are you doing yours?

And of course I am afraid, because the transformation of silence into language and action is an act of self-revelation, and that always seems fraught with danger. But my daughter, when I told her of our topic and my difficulty with it, said, "Tell them about how you're never really a whole person if you remain silent, because there's always that one little piece inside you that wants to be spoken out, and if you keep ignoring it, it gets madder and madder and hotter and hotter, and if you don't speak it out one day it will just up and punch you in the mouth from the inside."

In the cause of silence, each of us draws the face of her own fear—fear of contempt, of censure, or some judgment, or recognition, of challenge, of annihilation. But most of all, I think, we fear the visibility without which we cannot truly live. Within this country where racial difference creates a constant, if unspoken, distortion of vision, Black women have on one hand always been highly visible, and so, on the other hand, have been rendered invisible through the depersonalization of racism. Even within the women's movement, we have had to fight, and still do, for that very visibility which also renders us most vulnerable, our Blackness. For to survive in the mouth of this dragon we call america, we have had to learn this first and most vital lesson—that we were never meant to survive. Not as human beings. And neither were most of you here today, Black or not. And that visibility which makes us most vulnerable is that which also is the source of our greatest strength. Because the machine will try to grind you into dust anyway, whether or not we speak. We can sit in our corners mute forever while our sisters and our selves are wasted, while our children are distorted and destroyed, while our earth is poisoned; we can sit in our safe corners mute as bottles, and we will still be no less afraid.

Each of us is here now because in one way or another we share a commitment to language and to the power of language, and to the reclaiming of that language which has been made to work against us. In the transformation of silence into language and action, it is vitally necessary for each one of us to establish or examine her function in that transformation and to recognize her role as vital within that transformation.

For those of us who write, it is necessary to scrutinize not only the truth of what we speak, but the truth of that language by which we speak it. For others, it is to share and spread also those words that are meaningful to us. But primarily for us all, it is necessary to teach by living and speaking those truths which we believe and know beyond understanding. Because in this way alone we can survive, by taking part in a process of life that is creative and continuing, that is growth.

And it is never without fear—of visibility, of the harsh light of scrutiny and perhaps judgment, of pain, of death. But we have lived through all of those already, in silence, except death.

And I remind myself all the time now that if I were to have been born mute, or had maintained an oath of silence my whole life long for safety, I would still have suffered, and I would still die. It is very good for establishing perspective.

And where the words of women are crying to be heard, we must each of us recognize our responsibility to seek those words out, to read them and share them and examine them in their pertinence to our lives. That we not hide behind the mockeries of separations that have been imposed upon us and which so often we accept as our own. For instance, "I can't possibly teach Black women's writing—their experience is so different from mine." Yet how many years have you spent teaching Plato and Shakespeare and Proust? Or another, "She's a White woman and what could she possibly have to say to me?" Or, "She's a lesbian, what would my husband say, or my chairman?" Or again, "This woman writes of her sons and I have no children." And all the other endless ways in which we rob ourselves of ourselves and each other.

We can learn to work and speak when we are afraid in the same way we have learned to work and speak when we are tired. For we have been socialized to respect fear more than our own needs for language and definition, and while we wait in silence for that final luxury of fearlessness, the weight of that silence will choke us.

The fact that we are here and that I speak these words is an attempt to break that silence and bridge some of those differences between us, for it is not difference which immobilizes us, but silence. And there are so many silences to be broken.

WRITING SURVIVAL

valerie jean

Suicide is such a simple, even sweet-sounding, word, the way its easy rhythm curls the lips, its syllables falling almost hypnotic. *Suicide.* I have come to hate the word and the idea it conjures up of some romantic notion of noble human drama. There is nothing simple or sweet or even remotely romantic or noble about a person's decision to kill themselves. For those left behind, the word itself takes on an aching, overwhelming power and becomes a poisoned legacy. Terri L. Jewell committed suicide in November 1995, and I am still struggling to understand it, still wrestling with a grief. How do I begin to talk about her decision to put a gun to her head and pull the trigger? As a writer, I know I have to find the words, have to figure out some way to talk about the rage/silence her death has covered me with. This search is not just about words. This is about survival.

It feels so impossible, so difficult to explain. How to write through this grief? How to say what the language seems inade-

quate to express? How to remember Terri, remember Phyllis and countless others whose faces and names I do not know? How to admit the despair, the fear, the anger? How do I write about pain, the struggle to heal? What will keep me alive?

Terri had been dead for more than a month before I found out. We were writing buddies. We'd met only once, at the Audre Lorde CeleConference in Boston in October 1990. She had an idea for a newsletter to keep the "sisterspirit" we (about thirty to forty Black women who'd come together in a session there) had created among ourselves. She had talked about the joy she felt at our gathering and how isolated she was living in Michigan. She talked about us needing to keep in touch with each other. I suggested that she write letters and promised that if she wrote me, I'd write back. I don't remember if we even hugged then. It all feels so long ago.

Terri's death shook my soul to its core and threatened everything I'd learned to believe in. It caused me to stop writing. Yet here I am doing the work that I know is necessary, praying that my words are coherent, that my writing will somehow honor Terri's life and the love she brought into mine. I have to do this, because writing is what I do. It is how I survive. I write, and watch the sky. And every day I listen to the music of Sweet Honey in the Rock, and to the birds and plants when I walk. At night I try to gather stars and place them in a child's dream. I tell the stories I know, while the world sleeps.

Terri was my friend. We shared so many words, letters, between us. It was our love of writing letters that bound us together, made us sisters. We discovered page by page there were so many things we had in common. Our favorite color was purple. We both loved nature, the calmness of water, saw such beauty in the clouds. She told me about a "favorite place" of hers where she often went to write. I told her about "my" lake.

We vented to each other about our no-good-for-our-spirit jobs and helped each other maintain sanity in the craziness that surrounded us. We were both Black women poets who believed in the writing, in the power of words, our words, to make a difference, *or so I thought.* We both adored Audre Lorde, quoted her to each other. I remember Terri's trepidation and courage when she decided to go dread. She was concerned, too, about how we Black sisters survive in this country. *So why didn't she survive?*

She knew I was straight. I knew she was lesbian. It didn't matter. Between us, we wrote about what was important in our lives, the loves and the fears. She shared a good deal of her "madness" (as she called it) with me. I wrote her about my own struggles. Through our words, it seemed we could get deeper clarity about almost anything. I thought we both understood the power in our words. Terri wrote a lot about feeling isolated, even as she acknowledged the "life-saving power" in our letters. Over the course of our five-year conversation, she told me how she was getting along with her therapist, about her "coping" strategies and the prescribed drugs. She trusted me enough to share the source of a lot of her problems, the abuse she had suffered as a child, and she wrote me when she'd been diagnosed as manic-depressive. She wrote of her hospital stays, how they were necessary periods of renewal for her. And she was there for me to write out my own "madness." It is ironic, but it was Terri who most helped me get past the death of another friend.

The pain comes over me in waves, sometimes, still shakes me like the ocean smacking against the sand. Each time I remember something she said or I hear an ignorant comment about Black people and suicide, it's like a hammer upside my head and I want to scream.

I cannot talk about Terri's death without talking about Lorraine's. Their deaths are now intertwined in my heart. Lorraine was also my friend, but I'd walked away from her because she would not leave her abusive husband. Her death knocked down the walls of secrecy I'd spent many years building. None of my current friends knew Lorraine. I'd never talked about her. How could I talk about Lorraine and not admit my own abusive marriage, which I'd never talked about, either? Lorraine and I were connected in a past time that I feel ashamed of. When she died of a cocaine overdose in November 1994, I was overcome by both guilt and grief. I had not been there for her. I couldn't help but think that she'd chosen death as the only escape she could imagine from a situation she felt powerless to change—a kind of subtle suicide.

Terri was there for me while I grieved for Lorraine and began to confront my own still buried fears. In her letters, Terri wrote that I had to name the hurt, to speak it. She urged me to write down the pain and send it to her. She even convinced me to go see a therapist. The sister believed in "getting help for yourself, in doing whatever it takes" to get and be well. *I don't understand how she could not hear what she made me believe.*

Terri helped me begin to write about Lorraine and my own abuse. Writing *LPs (Recordings)*, the sixty-four poems that poured out about Lorraine, was a hard and demanding task. But it was also healing. Still, I was reluctant to share the work. Terri said the writing of it saved my life. She told me this was how we "poets" had to do it. She kept after me to "do the work" and kept nudging me to share it with her.

She never got a chance to see what she had helped me put on paper. She understood my fear about sharing the poems and was willing to wait. She seemed to understand everything. She wrote me a long letter sharing the suicides and painful circumstances of others she had known and lost. She told me what she did to survive. At the top of the list was Audre Lorde's solution. Terri summarized, "Write it down, girl. Tell everyone how much it hurts. Sharing will make it easier to bear." *It doesn't make sense how she showed me a way to survive and then she didn't.*

On January 2 I went to the post office to pick up my mail and was surprised to see that the package I'd sent her had been returned. I asked the clerk about it. I could not see the hand-written message: "Deceased 1288 12/26/96." The clerk must have thought I was dense. In her harried state, she pointed— "Here. It says 'Deceased.' She's gone"—and thrust the package back into my hands. I stood there, wanting to tell the clerk, "No. You don't understand. This package is important. Terri needs to get this mail," but no words came out. Inside there was a letter, a Sweet Honey tape, a couple of postcards, a spirit rock (the spider, symbolizing creativity), and the now twenty-six-poem manuscript about Lorraine, *LPs (Recordings)*.

I don't remember how I made it home that evening, but I do know that I called up several friends, told them what had happened, asked how I could find out for sure whether or not she was dead. My mind kept making up excuses. I thought maybe she went to see her parents, or maybe she was in the hospital again, or perhaps she forgot to tell me that she was going "on tour" promoting her books. *What did the clerk know?*

The next day I ran away. I had picked up *Sula* to read on the way downtown. I wasn't sure where I was going, I just needed to go, get out of the house, walk, be out of my life for a while. I didn't want to have to think about Terri, wonder what was going on with her, where she was, or have to talk to any of my friends about her. On the metro, trying to use *Sula* to distract myself, I came upon Morrison's character Shadrock, celebrating his unique holiday, "National Suicide Day." It stunned me when I realized that "today is January 3," and I knew then that Terri was dead. I closed the book, got off the metro, and just walked.

I walked the mall for a long time in the cold. My mind was muddled, frozen. After a couple of hours, I needed to get warm. I found myself at the only museum open that day, in line for tickets to an exhibition of Vermeer's paintings. There was a long line and wait. Even after getting my ticket, I had to wait a couple more hours before I was scheduled to go in. Unable to keep still, I returned to the blustering winds and walked some more. Finding myself near the library, thinking (or perhaps *not* thinking) I could find out something about Terri, I spent about an hour searching through Michigan newspapers, looking/not looking through obituaries.

That night I called several friends, expressing my uncertainty and denial. My heart told me she was dead, but I could not listen, didn't want to believe what I knew was true. I reread her chapbook, stopping at the "Missing Hymen" poem with the lines ". . . I hugged death / like a thick, blue blanket / its borders embroidered / with shiny new bullets / saved for the time / I could choose passage out . . ." and then I remembered that we had made an antisuicide pact. I reread all her letters to me to confirm this. She could *not* be dead!

A few days later, a journalist friend was able to contact the newspaper in Lansing and confirm what I knew. I did not know for sure how she had died, but I felt it was suicide. I stopped writing that day, though, thank God, I continued to talk to my friends and family. I knew I could not keep Terri's death inside me and live.

Her last letter to me was dated 11/10/95 and was full of the downside. She talked about her new medication, about how she missed her "manic" side, but was trying to trust that her therapist knew what she was doing. She was determined not to go into the hospital that year. For the last three years Terri had gone to the psychiatric ward of some hospital. Something about the fall, especially Thanksgiving, brought out the worst depressions in her. I'd send encouraging postcards and "Hey, where the hell are you?" notes until she got out and could write that she was okay and was all excited about the next project she wanted to work on.

Terri always seemed to have something she was working on. My God, did this woman work! Her chapbook *Succulent Heretics* had just come out in 1994. She'd edited a wonderful anthology of Black women's sayings, *Black Women's Gumbo Ya Ya*, which came out in 1993. She was in the midst of two important projects, one a Black lesbians engagement/calendar book, the other an anthology of personal accounts of why sisters go dread. She was so full of life and spirit, so energetic. But she was also struggling. In that last letter, she just asked me to listen. It was part of our pact, to put down the pain on the page.

Sometimes I still get so angry with her, find myself asking a door, an empty chair, or just staring out the window, "*Why?*" Sometimes I want to shake her or to slap the shit out of her, just to make her leave me alone. Sometimes I want to choke her to death, *but she is already dead. Her eyes invade my dreams, staring, wanting . . . what? She had agreed, "Yes, we could be sisters," and wrote that my letters were keeping her alive. She had promised me she wouldn't commit suicide, and then she broke that promise. And I can't ever tell her how awful that makes me feel.*

They say she died sometime after Thanksgiving. They don't have an exact date. She was found in her car on November 28. They are not sure how long her body had been there. Found her in her car, which was full of blood. Said she shot herself in the head in what sounded like that "most favorite" place she had described to me. But even before learning all the details, I knew it had been a violent death. Blood soaked my dreams. I would get up from the bed, not rested, and wonder how to make it through the rest of the night, another morning. Sometimes I would sit at the computer, or over my journal, and simply stare. My hands would shake. My whole body would shake. It felt as if my head were exploding.

What had always sustained me, had always been there, through everything else, what was most important to me as a poet—my words—had dissipated into thin air and were replaced by a sadness and a rage/silence that accompanied me everywhere. When Terri died, all my poetry vanished. How can I now explain the horror I felt when all the sounds, the images and their rhythms, just disappeared? The "screaming/silence" (how else can I name the noises that were so hollow echoing inside my skull) terrorized me. I still hear echoes some days, some nights. How do I articulate that nothingness that can still trample down my bones?

Over and over I pleaded with my friends, "Please . . . I cannot stand another sister dying." When I knew that Terri was gone, reaching out to my friends, all of them, helped me to survive. I even convinced myself that I was really doing okay. Terri had taught me that not talking about the pain was wrong. Unlike Lorraine's death, I did not keep Terri's death a secret. My friends and family were my strength, and I leaned heavily on them. I called up everyone, told them that I was grieving for Terri, told many of them about Lorraine for the first time. With their help and support, I figured I had everything covered and thought that I was going to be all right. But I was not hearing any poetry in my heart.

One month later I wrote an essay about my daughter turning twenty-one. I was ecstatic to have the writing return. I was "acknowledging the sad," as another friend told me I needed to. But I was not writing poetry, and I was feeling terribly distracted, unbalanced, inside. I knew something was wrong, but I ignored it. I kept thinking of what Terri would have encouraged me to do. She would have written, "Go and see somebody. Get yourself some help." Then I kept thinking of how she had been seeing somebody for years and how, obviously, that hadn't saved her.

When the panic attacks came and insomnia carried me through three days and nights, I felt myself moving toward the path Terri had chosen. I was mouthing to all my friends how I could not understand how Terri could do what she did, that I did not understand her desperation. But, inside, the despair was so loud, I could not hear the ache of my own heart. When her suicide started to make too much sense to me, I had to make a choice. With the encouragement of a good friend, I went to the doctor and asked for help. In the waiting room I made another conscious decision that I was not going to go out like Terri did. This became my mantra. I still chant it, sometimes, to calm a rising panic that slips up.

The antidepressants prescribed by the doctor got me up in the morning. The other medication helped me sleep and stopped the anxiety/panic. They were all I needed. Therapy was not going to kill me, like . . . I suffered through debilitating nightmares and days of insomnia. In daylight hours there were sightings of the dead around my door. Gray days settled even with the sun. I watched a lot of TV, reread old *Star Trek* novels, and couldn't stop eating. That was pretty much my life for the next couple of months—make it up in the mornings, take my medication, make it to work/through a day, watch TV, talk to my friends. I hungered for the poetry I'd always known, but I could hear no words, no melodies.

A lot of my friends encouraged me to apply to Cave Canem, a workshop/retreat for Black poets. One girlfriend even wrote my cover letter. But how could I be among poets when I was not sure I could call myself one anymore? In the end, I sent off the letter and required poems only because I did not want to disappoint my friends. I waited to be rejected.

But I was *invited* to be among them, one of twenty-seven Black poets. There, at Cave Canem, I rediscovered my voice. I heard it sung from the lips of several sister word-weavers and recognized it in the sudden wail of a brother poet. There I was, so sad, so disheartened, among so many beautiful, singing voices. Something within opened that week, and I could hear my own voice again and not be repulsed or ashamed. I heard my own voice as part of a necessary choir. I cannot describe what hearing the words re-form inside me felt like, but I felt them reentering my soul in the morning, on the songs of the birds, heard them echoed in the Hudson River rushing past. There, a deer looked me straight in the eye, and the stars spilled out of the sky like firecrackers in my heart. There I learned a new way of sharing my work, and it loosened my own choked-backed words.

At Cave Canem I thought of Terri often, of how she should have heard what I was hearing, how she should have waited for the chance to "sing" her own "songs" there. I read her poems to the fields and the river. I don't know where Terri is buried, but I visited the graveyard of priests and made a kind of peace with her spirit there.

I know my grieving for Terri is not done. There are sudden, bold moments that grab me, that I cannot control, but Cave Canem taught me that I could survive, that I must survive. The experience reminded me to always trust the words, to write down the pain. There, I learned how to recapture joy. It became so clear to me that if my words ever stopped coming, if the emptiness swells again, I have the hearts and the words of my brother and sister poets. Cave Canem gave me a community to feel safe in, where I could start letting go of some of the sadness. It taught me how to remember laughter and love. I think of Terri, think she would have survived, had she been there. She should have waited.

I have to believe that what I write is necessary healing and is not just about me and my pain, but will be useful to others. I don't want to hear about another friend, another Black woman or man, killing themselves. I struggle to accept Terri's and Lorraine's deaths even though I know they are both ancestor-spirits now. I know Terri will not write me any more letters. She did not believe in our words, their power, but I do. The universe lost a beautiful sister-poet. I lost a friend. But I am writing again, hearing poetry fill my soul. I want everyone to know that it is possible to get past any sorrow, and that it is worth it to *live*.

POET SONIA SANCHEZ

Telling What We Must Hear

juanita johnson-bailey

INTRODUCTION

With the unblinking and critical poet's eye, Sonia Sanchez has been setting her readers straight, telling the "terrible beauty," and reflecting images in ways that simultaneously solicit tears and laughter. For over thirty years this revolutionary poet has been undeterred from a path that began in the sixties when Black militancy was the vogue. Still, she has not given up the struggle to let her poetry be what she refers to as a "call to arms" for her people. But her people have not always responded with reciprocal dignity and purity of heart. So her way has at times been solitary, weary, joyful, and painful.

She has won numerous awards, including the prestigious PEN *Writing Award, a National Endowment for the Arts fellowship, the Lucretia Mott Award, an American Book Award, and an honorary doctorate in fine arts. Her latest book,* Wounded in the House of a Friend *(1996), follows a long, consistent line of such outstanding works as* Under a Soprano Sky *(1987),* Homegirls and Handgrenades *(1984),* A Blues Book for Blue Black Magical Women *(1978),* We a BaddDDD People *(1970), and* Homecoming *(1969). Her work also includes plays, children's books, short stories, and essays.*

In this conversation she moves between discussing her poems and artistry with a ready laugh and a fast staccato speech. Her words are audible in personal moments of active resistance, her mettle is evident in the stance of contemporary courageous Black women writers, and her truth ever echoes in her work—always militant, always radical, always challenging.

THE POETIC BEGINNINGS

I really think my first exposure to poetry was from my grandmother, who spoke in what we call Black dialect. My earliest remembrance is when I was around fourish. She would say things in a certain way, and I would repeat it. And she'd look up at me. I would kind of do it again, smile, go off in a corner someplace, and go on saying it. Some people felt that I was mocking her. I was not. It was just that something in my ear told me it was a brilliant way of saying it. So I would repeat it.

Grandmother knew books were important to me, and naturally we had a lot. I would always pick up a book, open it, and try to figure out what was being said. Either my grandmother or cousin Louise taught me how to read at four.

What I remember most is the love and respect my grandmother had for me. She knew that I was different. I already had figured out that I was odd; children figure that out at an early age. She said, "Just let the girl be. She be all right. She gonna stumble on her gentleness one of these days." Grandmother passed on the whole idea that I could do what I wanted to do. Women like her kept hopes and dreams alive in us. Once when I jumped out of a second-story window all she said to me is, "You okay?" And I said, "Yes." And she said, "Well, go on and play." She didn't grab me, even though I did have some bruises. She would shoo me out to do this world. And that's what I've been trying to do—this world.

My mother died giving birth to twins when I was one year old, and my grandmother died when I was six. The response to my grandmother's death made me tongue-tied, and after that I stuttered. This meant that people left me alone. So I started writing little things that everyone said were poems because they rhymed. I wrote because I stuttered and no one ever wanted to take the time to listen. I used to pass little notes; it was the way that I spoke.

One of the first little poems I did was to Walter, who was a terrible little boy, but I liked him and he liked me. I also wrote a poem about George Washington crossing the Delaware, which my sister found and read to the family. Everybody fell out laughing. After this I began keeping journals, which I couldn't hide in the bedroom that I shared with my sister. There is no privacy with a sister. Since it was my job to clean the bathroom every Saturday, it was no problem hiding my journals there. I stuck everything I was reading and writing underneath the tub, the kind with the raised legs. I would be sitting in there at three o'clock in the morning, writing.

I believe that I was born a poet. A lot of people are poetic but never really learn or nurture the craft. Therefore they'll write a poem once or twice a year. A college poetry teacher, Louise Bogan, told me two important things. First, she told me that a lot of people have talent, but they do nothing with it. The other thing she said is that you have to write on cue because if you wait for this muse to drop down on your shoulders, it might drop once a year. Therefore she made us write a poem a week. That's when I first got disciplined.

I ran across certain people growing up in New York City who helped me along the way. One of these people was Jean Blackwell Hutson, the curator at the Schomburg Library. I had finished school and needed a job. I read the ads in *The New York Times* for writers and sent samples. I got a telegram—that's what they used to do, send telegrams—that said, "You are hired." I jumped up and down and celebrated with some of my friends. Then I went to work. I had on my blue suit, my blue pumps, my blue bag, my white gloves, and my blue hat to let them [Whites] know that I knew how to go to work. In my purse I had money to eat lunch, money to get back home, and the telegram. They said report at nine o'clock. I got down there at eight-thirty. I handed the telegram to the woman secretary— and she said, in a soft voice, "All right, okay, have a seat." So I sat down with a magazine, and someone came and peeped around the corner, looked at me, and went back. Then another face came. Finally a man came and said, "We're sorry, but the job is taken." And I said, "I have a job here." And he said, "Well, the job is taken," like "Well, what's your damn problem?" I said, "But no one else has come in here except me. How could . . . ?" I was amazed. It was just that fast. The secretary was sitting there with her eyes downcast. And I said to his retreating back, "I am going to report you to the Urban League!"

I left so angry that I got on the train and, instead of getting off where I was supposed to, I ended up at 135th Street and Lenox Avenue. And all of a sudden here's this place. I am hot. I am sweaty. It said "Library" and I said, "Let me go in, pick up some books, and read." A guard outside made me sign in. I asked, "What kind of library is this?" and he said, "The Schomburg." And I said, "The Schomburg. What's the Schomburg? Is it special?" He said, "Well, why don't you ask the lady inside." Inside to the right was this glass area where Jean Hutson, the curator at the time, sat. I went over, gestured to her, and she came out. I asked, "What kind of library is this?" And she said, "This library contains all books by and about Black folks." And I said in my sharp, acerbic fashion, "Must not be many books in here, then."

She told me to sit down and she'd bring me some books. As I inched myself into a long table with all men sitting around it, they looked up at me. I was the only female there. She brought me *Their Eyes Were Watching God*, *Souls of Black Folks*, and *Up from Slavery*. I picked *Their Eyes Were Watching God* and started reading. Softly I said, "Oh, my God. Oh, my God. Look at this." The language was so beautiful. I read maybe a third of it. I went to Ms. Hutson and said, "This is a beautiful book." She said, "Yes, dear. Go read now." When I finished the book I stood up again and said, "Oooh, what a beautiful book." One of the men said, "Miss Hutson, will you please tell this young woman to stay still or leave." For an entire week I hung out at the Schomburg when I was supposed to be looking for a job. And Ms. Hutson fed me books. She asked, "Is there anything you like to read?" When I said gently, "Poetry," she sent me all the poets she knew. On the last day I said to her, "I have to go and look for a job. But one day my books will be in here." Years later, when I was a professor at Amherst College and I brought classes to the Schomburg, she would tell that story much more beautifully than I do, with a very funny smile on her face.

THE SISTER CIRCLE

I used to have trouble sometimes when I read my poetry. I took a lot of abuse. The first time I read in New York City, people just sat and looked at me. Some people booed 'cause I said, "I'm a Black woman poet." I'll never forget it. I wrote poems that were obviously womanist before we even started talking about it. Men would get up and go on about their business because they said I was reading only for women. So one day I said out loud, "My poetry is just as important as your poetry." It was at a huge conference. And I was not invited back to a major conference for three years.

In my head my audience has always been Black folks, Black women. I am not a revisionist. I don't say that I have always understood sisterhood. Most women are socialized not to believe a whole lot of loving things about women. My generation began to forge a new way of looking at the world. We began to say to each other, "I don't take your husband. You don't take my husband." We began to work in women's groups. So now I greet all women as sister. Some Black women get upset about that because they say, "White women are not your sisters." And I'll say, "Yeah, and a lot of Black women are not my sisters, either." The point is to understand that until we organize women in this country the way we should be organized, we are in a lot of trouble.

The premise that we are sisters brought me full circle, back to the church where my grandmother and the women called each other sister. My grandmother was the head deaconess in the church. So on Saturdays her sisters came to do the cooking and the talking. I would come in and slide behind the couch that sat away from the wall so they would not put me to work. The women would be in there snapping beans, peeling potatoes, and fixing up the ham. In the midst of their work they would start talking about people—about somebody beating up somebody. And they would say, "Well, we don't let that happen." I knew Mama (my grandmother) wanted me to hear this because I would snicker and she would shoot her eyes behind the couch. Her eyes said "If you want to hear this, you keep quiet."

I used to hear her say, "Well, that ain't right of Sister Smith to do that." And someone would say, "You know, she really ain't nice." Although they called her sister, they knew some of those sisters weren't sisters. So I'm not inventing anything new. I'm just picking up on the ideology of my grandmother that says simply "Yes, I will call you sister, but you gotta make yourself sister."

The things we heard in the conversations among the women taught us something. I learned to curse by listening to Miss Dixon, a friend of my stepmother. When Miss Dixon came to our house, my father would leave. He couldn't stand her because she drank and cursed. But I loved when Miss Dixon came. I knew I would learn another curse word. She would come in loudly and say, "Sonia, bring me some beer." I would open the beer, taste the foam, bring it to her, and listen to her tell stories.

Miss Dixon was a huge woman, a big woman, who had been in show business. And she was the one who taught me how to watch people. She would say, "Girl, you cannot get along on this earth without knowing who people are. You gotta listen to people. Hear what's coming out of their mouths and hear what's coming out of their bodies, and know what odors they have."

The first poem that I wrote to Miss (Mama) Dixon was in *Under a Soprano Sky*. It was about being downtown at City Hall when this man pulled his car up on the sidewalk and pulled his penis out and said, "Do you want some of this?" I'd been talking to African women from all over the world, and this man could only see me as a whore on Market Street. I called on my old friend Miss Dixon, and she said, "What you gonna say to this man? You better tell him what needs to be said, Sonia." And I did. Afterward I wrote the poem "style no. 1," which mentions her by name.

When I finished cutting him up with my mouth he turned red and drove off real fast. I laughed out loud on Market Street. And Miss Dixon said, "I bet you he will think twice about coming up to somebody else."

EXTENDING THE CIRCLE

Teaching a course on the Black woman taught me what it was to say "sister" to people. It was a very hard time for me; I had separated from my husband, Ethridge Knight, a poet, who was on drugs. The female students were driving me insane, always coming in for conferences. They needed help being Black women on a White campus. Jokingly I said, "We need a course called 'The Black Woman.' " And they said, "Teach it!" So I designed this course. But I had not put into that syllabus what happened after we were in there maybe the third or fourth week. This young woman stood up and said, "I hate all Black men." And she started to talk about incest. I hugged her, and we all collectively caught our tears. I instinctively began to talk to her and that weekend read every damn thing I could find on incest. And it became part of what we talked about forever.

I tried to write to those young sisters about what it was to love themselves. I wrote *We a BaddDDD People* that year. Ethridge tore up the finished manuscript for this book because he was not writing. When I found myself on the floor, trying to piece together this book, I knew it was time to leave. At that moment I understood why those sisters gathered in my grandmother's house every Saturday. Ostensibly it was to cook the meals to sell on Sunday to raise money for the church. But it was really where they passed on information to each other, where they helped each other, and where they passed on information to some little terrible kid sitting behind the couch. They were telling me how you don't let someone hit you twice.

One night I got a frantic call that a former student was climbing the walls. Some of the sisters and I went to her house. She had taken something because this man that she had married had come home and she smelled his former lovemaking as she was making love to him. She flipped. We pumped her full of coffee and walked her back to sanity. It was for her I wrote,

> *he poured me on*
> *the bed and slid*
> *into me like glass.*
> *and there was*
> *the sound of splinters.*

You can't put splinters back together, but that's what we did as sisters. Sisterhood is very important. That hood is a covering. Sisters make everything possible on this earth.

CALLING UP THE ANCESTORS

Because of women like Miss Dixon and Mama (my grandmother) I've always been in touch with our female ancestors. In that sense my work is spiritual. And most of the work has a history to it. I am always researching and then creating from that research. I carry the mamas, I carry the sisters, the women who were on the block being sold. I carry those first Africans who came to this country and must have screamed out at the gods.

But in spite of our oppression we have maintained our humanity. We might be in danger of losing it with this younger generation, so our work is very important. We must work hard to make them understand the history/herstory that we have in the world—the humanity and the love that we have. I say to young people, I did not fight all these years to pull these sisters out of history, to put African women back on the world stage, to write about them and teach about them to have you get on stage and act like a fool or to become sex objects on MTV. It is a constant fight at the university and all over the earth to bring African women on center stage again, out of people's homes where they have relegated us—always somebody's mammy—public or private.

When I started to read literature I realized we'd been taken off the world stage. I say to young people, I didn't write "Improvisation," which is about the middle passage and those sisters screaming when they are being sold on these American planks, for you to get on MTV in a state of undress, rub your crotch, or make believe you are making love to the microphone. When you know your history, it means you don't allow someone to come up and record your derriere while you shake it back and forth. You don't go across the floor, lapping up toward a man.

It hurt me to see a woman on television announce that a young Black woman had performed a sexual act in the middle of a dance floor and that later the guy turned her over to his posse. I wrote a poem based on this incident and read it at the

Bronx Community College to young African American and Latino women. They were returning students, and many of them had a child or two. I pulled out the proofs of *Wounded in the House of a Friend* and read the poem "Like." It begins:

LIKE

All i did was
go down on him
in the middle of
the dance floor
cuz he is a movie
star he is a blk/
man "live" rt off
the screen fulfilling
my wildest dreams.

They said, "That's just like Tenisha." Then somebody said, "Yeah." And someone said, "Ms. Sanchez, that's not right, is it?" And I said, "Sister, that has nothing to do with right. She went down on the young brother because she was ahistorical. When you have history, you don't ever embarrass yourself or your people on the planet Earth." I told them how at the turn of the century Black women started clubs because White women would not let them into their clubs. We were called whores and prostitutes because of our enslavement. We couldn't help it. It wasn't prostitution. They raped us. These Black women went to newspapers and said, "We're not whores, we're not prostitutes, we are church women, we are good women. You cannot denigrate us in the newspapers the way you have done." And now, I said, "You willingly denigrate yourself on TV." They cried and they said no one had ever told them that before.

One of the things I'm trying to pull on is our residual memory as women. Somebody has said something somewhere along the way to help us. We have just blocked it out. Education has blocked it out. You forget that you see. What I try to do with these young girls is to tell things we were told when they straightened our hair in the kitchen on Saturday nights.

We are in danger, great danger, of losing the memory that connects us, that keeps us alive. The thing that has sustained us as African people was that we had memories. The woman on the dance floor should have known what she was saying very distinctly, that "we [Black women] are immoral, promiscuous, and unreliable." But she was ahistorical.

Once, when I read that poem, a very middle-class woman said, "You know, I love your poetry, but you really shouldn't read a poem like that out loud. White people think we are all like that." And I said, "Yes, I should. They know we don't all take crack. But these incidents are reported in the news."

I took another idea from the newspaper—about a sister leaving her child at a crack house. I put it up on the bulletin board in my bedroom. Every morning I read it and cried. Later I wrote, "Memories. What happens with memories? Crack kills memories." And the second thing I wrote was, "Child. This will silence the child." Then I wrote, "Will silence the people also. That's why crack is here, to silence the people and to silence our memories."

Crack wounds. And that's what I said in *Wounded in the House of a Friend*. The title of that book is from Zachariah, and the whole section is about prophecy. "And what of these wounds, naked in our back? . . . For we have been wounded in the house of our friends." That's not just a personal house that we are wounded in. It is the house of America that has allowed this to happen. But as Africans we are also wounded in our private houses, our bodies. When you bring crack into Black neighborhoods, it makes you forget all memories of yourself. So in "Poem for Some Women," about the young woman selling her daughter for crack, she couldn't even remember her daughter's name or what she looked like. Crack will kill memories so you *can* sell a daughter, give her up as a virgin. People dealing crack might not take it, but they also lose their memories and their history.

The first line of "Poem for Some Women" is "Huh?" And I started off on that level because it had to be a question mark. There was nothing that was final there. The woman's voice had to be first. It was not going to be my voice.

In telling, I try to give Black people strength, power, and a sense of themselves—who they are—who they must be—and what they must do during the short period they're on this earth. I try to make my people laugh, at the same time to teach and inform, to make us know and feel our beauty.

And another goal of my writing has been to reconcile us with ourselves and to reclaim our history/herstory. We must understand that before we can move on. Although we think we do it without them, some ancestor is pushing us. The title *Wounded in the House of a Friend* came at three o'clock in the morning while I was asleep. I woke up and wrote down the title. You see, our ancestors will wake us up in the middle of the night if we are not on time.

Poetry has kept me connected to this long line of African people who stayed alive just to tell their stories. I understand why I keep doing this work. It is part of a long tradition. It is what I am supposed to do. Writing poetry has kept me alive. It kept me breathing. It kept me human. It kept me a woman. It kept me from killing people. It kept me from killing myself.

POEM FOR FLIGHT

becky birtha

There will come a day—
it is not far off now—
when you wake in the morning and know
you were meant to be happy
and that you want it
more than you want
things, or memories
any concrete place called home
all the strings of the past that fasten you,
more than you want
justice or pride:
your old clay image of yourself
or the faint chance
that all that has gone wrong
may still change.

It is you who hold
the power to change.

And whatever it is that holds you
whatever it is you think you cannot live without
the time has come to open your hands and
let it go.
Run
flee
disappear
break loose
take wing

fly by night
move like a meteor
be gone.

If you fear it will never be possible
think of Harriet
who traveled alone
the first time
who finally freed three hundred people
but first
had to free
herself.

CONTRIBUTORS

Brenda Faye Bell is the director of the Piney Woods YMCA Satellite Site in Chattanooga, Tennessee. She is a poet, mother, grandmother, and foster parent.

Patricia Bell-Scott, daughter of Dorothy Wilbanks and big sister to Brenda Faye Bell, has written and taught about Black women's lives for two decades. A professor of child and family studies and women's studies at the University of Georgia, she is contributing editor to *Ms.* magazine, cofounding editor of *SAGE: A Scholarly Journal on Black Women,* and editor of three previous books.

Becky Birtha, a Black lesbian feminist Quaker mother, is the author of two short-story collections, *For Nights Like This One: Stories of Loving Women* and *Lover's Choice,* and a book of poetry, *Forbidden Poems.* She received an individual fellowship in literature from the Pennsylvania Council on the Arts in 1985 and a Creative Writing Fellowship Grant from the National Endowment for the Arts in 1988.

Harriet Ann Buckley, whose work is featured on the cover of this anthology, is a storyteller artist who lives in Memphis, Tennessee. She graduated from the Memphis College of Art and creates in many mediums, including watercolor, oil, fabric, leather, metal, and paper.

Pearl Cleage is an Atlanta-based writer whose works include the plays *Flyin' West, Blues for an Alabama Sky,* and *Bourbon at the Border;* two books of essays, *Mad at Miles* and *Deals with the Devil and Other Reasons to Riot;* and a novel, *What Looks Like Crazy on an Ordinary Day.*

Miriam DeCosta-Willis, professor of African American Studies at the University of Maryland Baltimore County, teaches African American, Caribbean, African, and Latin American literature. She has edited six books, including *The Memphis Diary of Ida B. Wells, Erotique Noire/Black Erotica,* and the forthcoming *The Art of Moréjon.*

Ruth Forman, an award-winning writer and filmmaker, lives in Los Angeles. She is the author of *We Are the Young Magicians* and the forthcoming *Renaissance.* Widely anthologized, her work has been shared in a variety of forums such as the United Nations, the National Black Arts Festival, National Public Radio, and the Public Broadcasting Service.

Marcia Ann Gillespie, writer-activist, is editor in chief of *Ms.* magazine and former editor of *Essence.*

Marita Golden, a faculty member in the Graduate Creative Writing Program at Virginia Commonwealth University, is the author of the memoir *Migrations of the Heart* and three novels, including *Long Distance Life.* She also edited the anthology *Wild Women Don't Wear No Blues.*

bell hooks is Distinguished Professor of English at City College, City University of New York. She is a writer, feminist theorist, and cultural critic. She is the author of twelve books, the most recent of which are *Killing Rage: Ending Racism, Bone Black: Memories of Girlhood,* and *Wounds of Passion.*

Anita F. Hill is a professor of law at the University of Oklahoma Law School and coeditor of *Race, Gender and Power in America: The Legacy of the Hill-Thomas Hearing.*

Akasha (Gloria) Hull, a poet-critic-teacher and professor of women's studies and literature at the University of California, Santa Cruz, is completing a book on African American women's spirituality.

Valerie Jean, a poet, undeniably Black and woman, graduated with a master's of fine arts from the University of Maryland in College Park in 1989. Her work has been published in various journals and anthologies.

Juanita Johnson-Bailey self-defines as a daughter, spouse, mother, and Black feminist researcher. An assistant professor of adult education and women's studies at the University of Georgia, she is completing a book on Black reentry college women.

Audre Lorde was a Black feminist lesbian warrior poet mother who authored nine volumes of poetry and five works of prose. The recipient of many distinguished honors, including honorary doctorates from Hunter, Oberlin, and Haverford Colleges, she was named New York State Poet in 1991. Her personal writings are a source of inspiration for women around the world. She died of cancer in 1992.

Robbie McCauley is a performance artist, writer, and teacher whose works reflect the struggles and triumphs of African Americans under apartheid. She won a Bessie Award in 1990 for *Sally's Rape: The Whole Story*, a drama that used the relationship of Sally Hemmings, a Black slave woman, and Thomas Jefferson as a prism through which to examine historical and contemporary events. She also appeared on Broadway in Ntozake Shange's *for colored girls who have considered suicide when the rainbow is enuf.*

Wini "Akissi" McQueen is a textile artist who designs and dyes art wear for everyday use. In 1988 she began making narrative quilts about families, communities, and notable people using photo-fabric art techniques. Her quilts have been exhibited at the Museum of American Folk Art, the Taft Museum, the Bernice Steinbam Gallery, and the Williams College Art Museum. She is the two-time recipient of the Georgia Council for the Arts Award and voted among the fifty most influential women in the arts in Georgia. She also received a Lila Wallace Reader's Digest Grant to document the narrative tradition of textiles in the Ivory Coast. She is a 1968 graduate of Howard University.

Nell Irvin Painter, Edwards Professor of American History at Princeton, is author of *Sojourner Truth: A Life, A Symbol* and three other books of history.

Kate Rushin was raised in Camden and Lawnside, New Jersey. She graduated from Oberlin College and holds a master of fine arts in creative writing from Brown University. Her book of poems, *The Black Back-Ups*, was named a Book of the Teen Age in 1994 by the New York Public Library. Currently she is the director of the Center for African American Studies at Wesleyan University.

Sonia Sanchez, a poet, essayist, and playwright, holds the Laura Carnell Chair in English at Temple University. She is the author of numerous books, among which are the recently released *Wounded in the House of a Friend* and *Does Your House Have Lions?*

Sapphire is a performance poet and author of the award-winning novel *Push* and a collection of poetry, *American Dreams*. She earned a master of fine arts from Brooklyn College and lives in New York.

Elaine Shelly is a writer and performance artist. Her journal entries were published in the collection *Life Notes: Black Women's Personal Writings*, edited by Patricia Bell-Scott. She is completing her first novel, *Loving to the Bone*.

Barbara Smith, writer, independent scholar, and activist, is cofounder of Kitchen Table: Women of Color Press, coeditor of *The Reader's Companion to U.S. Women's History*, and author of numerous books and essays. She is writing the first history of African American lesbians and gays in the U.S.

Gilda Snowden, artist, curator, and writer, is an associate professor of painting at the Center for Creative Studies, College of Art and Design in Detroit. She is also gallery director of the Detroit Repertory Theatre. Her work has been exhibited and is part of many corporate and museum collections, including the Detroit Institute of Arts.

Sojourner Truth, whose given name was Isabella, was born about 1799 in Ulster County, New York, to James and Elizabeth Bomefree. She is perhaps the most widely known Black woman of the nineteenth century. Although she never learned to read and write, she dictated and published her life as *The Narrative of Sojourner Truth.*

Alice Walker won the Pulitzer Prize and the National Book Award for her novel *The Color Purple.* She has authored several novels, children's books, and collections of short stories, poetry, and essays. Born in Eatonton, Georgia, she now lives in Northern California.

Dorothy Graves Wilbanks, mother of Patricia Bell-Scott and Brenda Faye Bell, lives in Chattanooga, Tennessee. A retired telephone operator, she has begun quilting again, an avocation she learned from her grandmother and mother.